Introduction to Thomistic Philosophy

John Peterson

University Press of America,® Inc.
Lanham • Boulder • New York • Toronto • Plymouth, UK

Copyright © 2013 by University Press of America,® Inc.
4501 Forbes Boulevard, Suite 200, Lanham, Maryland 20706
UPA Aquisitions Department (301) 459-3366

10 Thornbury Road, Plymouth PL6 7PP, United Kingdom

All rights reserved
Printed in the United States of America
British Library Cataloguing in Publication Information Available

Library of Congress Control Number: 2012946005
ISBN: 978-0-7618-5986-4 (paper : alk. paper)—ISBN: 978-0-7618-5987-1 (electronic)

∞™ The paper used in this publication meets the minimum requirements of American National Standard for Information Sciences Permanence of Paper for Printed Library Materials, ANSI/NISO Z39.48-1992.

To James, Donald, Gloria, Marco,
Maggie, Eleanor, Mary, and Clara

Contents

Acknowledgments		vii
1	Metaphysics and Being	1
2	God	19
3	Teleology	35
4	Truth, Knowledge and Goodness	49
5	Persons	69
6	Ethics	91
7	Universals	119
Index		129

Acknowledgments

I am grateful to my colleagues in philosophy at the University of Rhode Island for their support and encouragement. I am especially indebted to Fritz Wenisch for his insights in regard to several of the philosophical issues which I discuss in these chapters. Thanks are also due to my former colleagues William Young and Stephen Schwarz who never grew tired of my questions over the years, and who were eager to philosophize at any moment. Last but not least, I cannot say how much I owe to my wife Mary for all her support, encouragement and patience.

Chapter One

Metaphysics and Being

THE COMPASS OF PHILOSOPHY

Sciences are distinguished by their objects. This is just to say that they are many because they concern different things. Biology studies living things, anthropology studies human beings, and so on. They each of them cut off a part or a portion of being and study just that part or portion and no other. Sometimes they study the same object but do so from different points of view. Sociology, history and anthropology all study humans but do so from different standpoints. In scholastic terminology, all three sciences have the same material object but differ as to their formal objects.

With what part or type of being does philosophy deal? The answer varies with the branch of philosophy. One such branch, epistemology, deals directly with knowledge, belief, and truth. Every major issue and question in epistemology focuses on one or more of these three concepts. Moreover, to the extent that knowledge, belief, and truth depend on and happen to be found in the minds of persons, it might be said that epistemology incidentally deals with minds and persons.[1] In other words, one can say that epistemology considers minds and persons indirectly because what it directly considers, i.e. knowledge, belief, and truth, depend on and exist in the minds of persons. In any case, about all three concepts a number of basic questions arise and these questions comprise the subject-matter of epistemology. Included in these questions are: What is belief? What is knowledge and how does it differ from true belief? What is the relation of knowledge and truth? What is the scope and what are the limits of our knowledge? What is the definition of truth? What is the bearer of truth? What is the test or criterion of truth?

Another branch of philosophy, ethics, deals with value concepts like rightness and goodness. And more specifically it concerns goodness in persons and the rightness or wrongness of their actions. The former is called virtue-ethics and the latter duty ethics. A meta-ethical question is how these are related in terms of priority. Are right actions defined in terms of a virtuous character from which they spring or is a virtuous character defined in terms of right actions? In any case, since moral goodness and right or wrong actions are found in persons, it can be said that ethics too deals incidentally with persons. But its direct object is not persons as such, but persons considered solely from the standpoint of the value of their characters and actions.

Ethics is thus both a normative and a practical science. As to the former, it measures the character and actions of persons according to a certain norm of goodness and of action. And as to the latter, it is knowledge not for the sake of knowledge but for the sake of action. Ethics finally aims at *being* a good person and *acting* rightly. It does not have as its final end simply knowing what makes a person a good person and what makes an action a right action.[2]

Third is logic which concerns principally that type of being which we call reasoning or argument. And once again, since these are found only in persons, it can be said that logic, like epistemology and ethics, deals incidentally with persons. It indirectly deals with persons because what it directly focuses on, i.e. arguments, are found only in persons. Moreover, to distinguish logic from psychology (which among other things might also consider the arguments of persons) it must be added that logic deals with arguments only from a certain point of view, namely, from the standpoint of their being either correct or incorrect. By argument or reasoning, we move from what is more evident to us to what is less evident to us. And as we do this either well or badly, logic, like ethics, is a normative science. It adjudicates the correctness or incorrectness of arguments according to certain norms. As ethics judges whether our actions are right or wrong, so logic judges whether our thinking is right or wrong. And to do either one, one must appeal to and to apply norms of acting and of thinking, respectively. Finally, the aim of logic is true conclusions. We reason in order to reach true conclusions. That being the case, logic addresses the following question: how are our arguments to be structured so that, from true premises, we reach true conclusions? This question is behind both deductive and inductive logic. When it is deduction that is concerned, it takes the following form: how, starting with true premises, should we so structure our arguments that our conclusions follow *necessarily* from those premises? When it is induction that is concerned, it is this: how, again beginning with true premises, should we so structure our arguments that we reach conclusions that follow *probably* from our premises? This shows that logic is useful to us since in any field of inquiry we strive to advance from what is more easily known to what is less easily known. But moving from premises to conclusions is just how we make this transition. Yet though logic is useful to us in this way, it is not a practical science like ethics since its final end is not action but knowledge, i.e. knowledge of conclusions. Thus, while all practical sciences like ethics are normative sciences, not all normative sciences are practical sciences, logic being the obvious exception.

Fourth there is metaphysics. Unlike any other science and unlike the other three branches of philosophy that were mentioned, metaphysics does not deal with some specific type of being. Instead, its object is being taken just as being. In that way does metaphysics get behind every other science. The idea of living being or of human being evidently includes the idea of being, but not *vice versa*. Therefore, metaphysics, which deals with being as being, is logically prior to biology, anthropology, or for that matter every other natural or social science. But the idea of being is also included in the ideas of knowledge, belief, truth, moral goodness, right action, and argument, but again not *vice versa*. So metaphysics also logically precedes the other three branches of philosophy that were mentioned, i.e. epistemology, ethics, and logic. As the simple is logically prior to the composite, metaphysics is logically prior to every other science. It is, as the scholastics called it, first speculative science, first in the order of logic if not in the order of learning.

To say that the object of metaphysics is being as being means that metaphysics considers what enters into the idea of any real being taken just as a being. By analogy, the ideas of animal and of rational enter into a person taken just as person, and the ideas of living and of substance enter into any given organism such as a tree or a toad. Aristotle thought that when a being is considered not as being but as mobile, form and matter enter into that being as basic elements or principles.[3] Thus, to the extent that I am a changing being, I am composed of form and matter. The simple reason for this is that change implies both a substrate (matter) which undergoes change and a new attribute, state, or condition (form) which that substrate takes on. If then, form and matter are required for something to be a *mobile* being, what is required for something to be a being, *period*? This seems to be the leading question of metaphysics when metaphysics is construed as first speculative science.

And yet, this question harbors difficulties which the others do not. You can ask what goes into a being taken as person, as organism, or even more broadly, as mobile. But to ask what goes into a being just as being sparks a dilemma. Either what belongs to a being as being is something or it is nothing. If nothing, then there are no principles of being as being and metaphysics is a hoax. If something, then since that something is evidently being, then metaphysics is circular. For then one says that what explains a being taken just as being is being. In either case, the supposed cardinal question of metaphysics, i.e. what belongs to any being taken just as being, turns out to be nonsensical. Second, even if it makes sense, it seems that this most basic question of metaphysics hangs on another. To the question, "What belongs to a being just as being"? one answers differently depending on, say, whether one is a materialist or a non-materialist. The former, who believes that all there is is spatial-temporal, answers that being spatial belongs to any being just as being. But the latter, who disbelieves that all there is is in space-time, denies that answer. So the trouble is that the supposed basic question of metaphysics hangs on a more basic one.

Third, apart from problems with its basic question, metaphysics faces criticism as regards its object. Metaphysics studies being but is confined to no individual being and to no type or species of being. But every individual being as well as every type or species of being is being. So it seems that metaphysics studies everything, every individual being as well as every type or species of being. But a science that studies anything and everything studies nothing. By analogy, a shoe store that specializes in all types and styles of shoes specializes in no kind or style of shoe at all. Thus, being alleged to be about all objects, metaphysics is for that reason about no object. But then it is a pseudo-science.

Fourth, aside from problems with its object and central question, metaphysics is widely challenged on account of its method. The method of metaphysics departs from that of any one of the natural and social sciences. In the latter, verification is by means of observation and experimentation. Claims are adjudicated by appeal to sense experience. Not so in metaphysics. Typical metaphysical claims are neither verifiable nor falsifiable by appeal to sense experience. Suppose that it is claimed that reality as a whole is one and not many, or that it is not one but is comprised of many independent monads. Or suppose that it is claimed that the soul is immortal or that the self as it is in itself is free, or that the set of all caused things or events has a cause that is uncaused, and so on. How or by what method are these metaphysical claims verified if, as is evidently the case, they are not verified by appeal to experience? If, with the logical positivists, we make such empirical verification a condition of the meaningfulness of synthetic statements, then it follows that these and other metaphysical assertions are neither true nor false but plainly meaningless.

Fifth, it was said that while other sciences cut off a part or portion of being and make it an object of inquiry, metaphysics eschews any such precision. For *vis a vis* every other science, theoretical or practical, metaphysics is broad and all-encompassing in its point of view. Its object is being in general or being as such and not any one type of being. That implies that the idea of being as such is the widest genus of which the objects of the other sciences are species. If plants, the object of botany, is one type of being and humans, the object of anthropology, is another type or species of being, and so on, then that of which they are species, being in general, is evidently the genus and in fact the widest possible genus.

And yet, so far from being an advantage, this synoptic vision of metaphysics as over against the narrower scope of the special sciences seems to be inherently flawed. If being as such is the widest genus, then since difference is outside genus, then any difference in being comes from outside being. Thus, if animal is the genus of human, then the difference in this case, i.e. rational, is evidently outside of the genus animal. But it is impossible to cite a difference that is outside the genus when the latter is being. For outside of being is nothing. So if being as such is the widest genus, then it is a genus without difference, in which case being is a genus without any species. But the ideas of genus, difference, and species being correlative, this is impossible. So the irony is this: to distinguish itself from every other science, metaphysics must make its object being in general. Yet it seemingly cannot do this without making being the widest genus, something which it is impossible to do. So the very idea of metaphysics is impossible.

Sixth, metaphysics has been attacked for its impracticality. Almost every other science has a use or in some way serves our needs. Metaphysics, though, has no use or practical application. Spaceships cannot be built without applying our knowledge of mathematics and physics. Diseases cannot be cured or treated without applying our knowledge of biology, chemistry, anatomy, medicine, and so on. Hurricanes cannot be predicted without our knowledge of meteorology, and so on. The settlement of a metaphysical issue, however, makes no difference to our practical lives. What practical difference does it make whether or not there are universals, whether or not all difference is part of a larger Unity or Absolute, whether or not to be is to be perceived, and so on? Pragmatists like William James have argued that if it makes no practical difference which side of these or other metaphysical issues is true, then the sides in question are really no different. If there is no difference in theory which does not imply a difference in practice, says he, and if there is no practical difference in the sides to a metaphysical question, then it follows that those issues, and hence metaphysics itself, make no sense. For example, if it makes no practical difference whether there are or there are not universals, then there is no theoretical difference between the two assertions, "There are universals" and "It is not the case that there are universals." But if not, then the metaphysical question, "Are there or are there not universals"? becomes pointless. And if pointlessness implies a kind of meaninglessness, it follows that this as well as every other metaphysical question is meaningless.

Some of these objections apply to ethics and epistemology as well as to metaphysics. So if they are credible, then they undermine philosophy as a whole a well as metaphysics. For example, under the fourth objection, ethical and epistemological questions and statements are made as meaningless as metaphysical statements and questions. Take the celebrated puzzle of the criterion which is traced to the ancient Roman skeptic Pyrrho (c.361 – c.270 B.C.). To tell the true from the false requires a criterion. But to know if the criterion is a good one, one needs to know if it successfully picks out the true from the false. But this one cannot know unless one already knows the true from the false. Epistemologists from Pyrrho to the present have asked how this conundrum is to be solved. Yet if the positivists are right and all meaningful puzzles and questions are empirically verifiable, then it follows that this problem of the criterion is a meaningless puzzle. Or if the last objection is valid, then the problem of the criterion lacks meaning due to its impracticality. How we solve the problem, if we solve it at all, makes no practical difference to us either individually or as a society. Or take the question of whether we know reality itself or appearance, i.e. reality only as colored by our cognitive structures or categories. Once again, if either the fourth or the last objection is valid, then this epistemological question becomes senseless.

Moreover, the fourth objection, if valid, also undermines ethics. One basic question in ethics is whether things are good because we desire them or whether we desire them because they are good. Another is whether actions are right because we approve of them or whether we approve of them because they are right. A third is whether the rightness of actions is defined in terms of the goodness of their consequences or not. Since none of these questions are settled empirically, it follows, if the fourth objection holds, that none of these questions are meaningful.

All these objections to metaphysics can be answered. And in so doing not just metaphysics but philosophy itself is vindicated. As to the first objection, i.e. that the question, "What belongs to a being just as being"? spawns a hopeless dilemma and so is a senseless question, the answer is to take the dilemma by its first horn. True, what belongs to a being just as a being is either being or nothing. But to say that it is being is not to say that the leading question of metaphysics is circular. It is not a case of explaining being in terms of being. The reason is that in "What belongs to a being taken just as a being" 'being' refers to something different in the predicate than it does in the subject. In the subject it refers to being in the sense of a concrete substance, such as a particular tree or toad. But in the predicate it refers both to being in the sense of that by virtue of which a substance is what it is, i.e. essence, and to that by virtue of which there is a substance to begin with, i.e. existence. Thus the key to fielding the objection that metaphysics is circular for the reason given is to insist (with Aristotle) that 'being' is said in many senses and to distinguish (with Aquinas) that, of these senses, being in the sense of essence and being in the sense of existence are most basic.

As to the second objection, it might be true that one answers the question, "What belongs to a being just as being"? differently depending on whether one is a materialist or a non-materialist. But from that it hardly follows that the prior question in metaphysics is not "What belongs to a being just as being"? but instead, "Is all there is in space"? To think that it does is to place the cart before the horse. Answering the second question partly answers the first, but answering the first does nothing to answer the second. For example, if all there is is in space, then being in space is one thing that belongs to a being just as being. But if we say that essence and existence belong to any being just as being, that answers the first question without shedding light on the second. If I know that any being just as being both is and is some sort of thing, then it remains an open question whether it is spatial or non-spatial. That shows that the broader, more fundamental question of metaphysics is "What belongs to a being just as being"? not, "Is all there is in space"?

As to the third objection, it is evident that it feeds on the fallacy of the half-truth. It is in one sense true that a science that studies anything and everything studies nothing. It is true when "anything and everything" refers to any and every rock, human, insect, tree, etc. taken just as rock, human, insect, tree, etc. But it is evidently not with anything and everything in this sense that metaphysics deals. Instead and as was said, metaphysics deals with rocks, humans, insects, trees, etc. *taken just as beings* and states that what belongs to any and every one of these things taken as beings or substances are the ultimate principles of beings or substances, such as essence and existence.

The fourth or positivist objection was met almost as soon as it was voiced. For why should it be assumed that philosophical claims are entirely unverifiable just because they are not *empirically* verifiable. To assume this is to reduce philosophy to science, to force philosophy into the mold of science. But why in the first instance should philosophy abandon its method of reason in favor of the method of sense verification? How can this demand be construed as anything else but arbitrary and simplistic? Not just that, but it was noted that the positivist position boomerangs on itself. The cardinal positivist principle that all meaningful non-analytic statements are empirically verifiable is *itself* empirically unverifiable and hence, by the positivist's own standard, meaningless.

The fifth objection is neutralized by distinguishing different senses of 'being.' Recall that that objection ran as follows. To say that other sciences focus on types of being whereas metaphysics studies just being implies that the object of metaphysics, just being, is the widest genus. For types or species of anything whatever are by definition types or species of a genus. Yet to account for types of being, the idea of being cannot possibly be the widest genus. Otherwise, since difference is outside of genus and outside of being is non-being, then nothing serves as a difference. So if being is the widest genus, then there could not in the first instance be various types of being, since all types or species include difference along with genus. Therefore, to the extent that it is defined as the science of being as being as over and against some type of being, metaphysics is contradictory.

The answer to this is not to follow Parmenides and conclude that being is one and that all difference is appearance. It is once again to distinguish senses of 'being.' When it is said that the special sciences study different types of being whereas metaphysics deals with just being, 'being' here has the sense of substance. The various sciences do study different types of substances, as, for example, biology studies living substances. And this does imply that being *in the sense of substance* is the widest genus. The object of metaphysics, then, is the widest genus, i.e. substance as such and not this or that type of substance. But unlike the vaguer notion of being, the idea of substance is not one outside of which there is nothing at all. The idea of an accident, for example, is outside the idea of substance. Therefore, when being means substance, one compatibly says both that the special sciences study different types of being whereas metaphysics studies just being.

The sixth objection fares no better than the rest. Just because it makes no practical difference whether one side of a philosophical issue is true rather than the other, why does it follow that the issue in question is spurious? Once again it follows only if one accepts an undefended assumption, i.e. the belief of pragmatists that all theoretical differences come down to, and are defined in terms of, practical differences. This in turn rests on the belief, first enunciated by Peirce, that the meaning of any predicate P comes down to how you would empirically test or show that something exemplifies P.[4] But besides being unproven, this dictum again boomerangs on itself. For under this assay, the meaning of "P means a rule of verification" comes down to how you empirically show that the predicate here belongs to the subject. But since there is no way in which it is empirically shown that "meaning a rule of verification" belongs to P, it follows that the pragmatist principle of meaning is by its own standard meaningless. To this pragmatists might reply that their dictum, "P means a rule of verification" applies only when P is outside of the definition of S. Therefore, the dictum fails to apply to itself since "P means a rule of empirical verification" is analytic or true by definition. But in that case, it cannot be charged after all that the pragmatist dictum is self-defeating or boomerangs on itself. Nevertheless, the evident counter reply to this is that pragmatists shield their principle from the charge of being self-defeating only by rendering it arbitrary. For why should anyone believe that it is simply a matter of definition that the meaning of any predicate whatsoever is identified with how you show empirically that something exemplifies that predicate? For on the face of it, this seems to confuse two questions. "What does P mean"? is different from and so cannot be reduced to asking, "What is the test for something's having the predicate P"?

Metaphysics and philosophy having been defended against some standard objections, the relation between the two must be further specified. In particular, how are the other main branches of philosophy, i.e. epistemology, logic, ethics, aesthetics, etc., related to metaphysics? Part of the answer to this question has already been given. It is that while metaphysics studies being just as being, the other branches of philosophy cut off some part or type of being and study that part and no other. In this, they are like the specialized sciences which do the same. For example, biology studies being only as living, anthropology studies being only as human, and so on. Similarly, epistemology cuts off a sphere of being and studies it and no other. It studies knowledge, belief and truth. Since all three are being but being is not necessarily any one of the three, epistemology, like the specialized sciences, is narrower than metaphysics. Yet it is important to see that epistemology is wider than any one of the specialized sciences. It takes its cue from metaphysics in its generality. For while each and every one of the specialized sciences considers only some particular area or domain of knowledge, belief, or truth, epistemology studies knowledge, belief and truth just as such. Thus, any knowledge, belief or truth in biology is knowledge, belief or truth just about living things, and any knowledge, belief, or truth in anthropology is knowledge, belief or truth just about humans, and so on. By contrast, the objects of epistemology are knowledge, belief and truth just as such and in themselves. When epistemologists ask what knowledge, truth and belief are, they are not asking what areas or domains of knowledge, belief or truth there are, such as knowledge of planets, beliefs about economics, or truths about whales. Still less are they focusing on just one of these specific areas of knowledge, belief or truth. They are asking about the concepts that enter into all three of the phrases, 'knowledge of planets,' 'beliefs about economics' and 'truths about whales,' namely, the concepts of knowledge, belief and truth themselves. And that these three concepts are more fundamental than the ones into which they enter is shown by the fact alone that the latter logically include them but not *vice versa*. Knowledge neither is nor includes knowledge of planets or else all knowledge is knowledge of planets. Belief neither is nor includes beliefs about economics or else all belief is belief about economics. And truth neither is nor includes truth about whales or else all truth is truth about whales. However and as was said, the ideas of knowledge, belief and truth *are* included in the ideas of knowledge of planets, belief about economics and truths about whales, respectively. So even though epistemology is narrower than metaphysics, it nonetheless qualifies as belonging to philosophy rather than the specialized sciences because of its generality. For it is to those special sciences what metaphysics is to it. As the object of metaphysics, being, is included in the objects of epistemology, i.e. knowledge, belief and truth but not *vice versa*, thus showing the logical priority of metaphysics to epistemology, so too are the objects of epistemology, i.e. knowledge, belief and truth included in the objects of any and all of the specialized sciences but again not *vice versa*, thus showing the logical priority of epistemology to any one of those specialized sciences.

The same holds for the relation between any one of the other branches of philosophy and metaphysics on the one hand and the specialized sciences on the other. They too, like epistemology, are narrower and less basic than metaphysics but yet wider and more basic than the specialized sciences. Take logic which studies arguments from the standpoint of their correctness. Arguments are beings of a sort; they are not nothing. Yet not all being is argument. So since being and the principles thereof are included in arguments but not *vice versa*, then logic is narrower and less basic than metaphysics. Nevertheless, as a branch of philosophy, logic is wider and more basic than any one of the specialized sciences. That is because logic considers arguments just in themselves and only from the viewpoint of their correctness. It is not confined to arguments in politics, arguments in religion, arguments in economics, arguments in biology, or what not. Practitioners in all of the specialized sciences use arguments to demonstrate their beliefs. But a logician does not use any one of the specialized sciences to show the correctness or incorrectness of any argument at all, even an argument that occurs in one of those sciences. The idea of an argument is included in the idea of an argument in politics or in any other field, but the idea of an argument in politics or the idea of an argument in any other field neither is nor is included in the idea of an argument. Otherwise all argument is identified with argument in politics or with argument in religion or with argument in biology, etc. Once again, just as it is in the case of the relation of epistemology to the specialized sciences, this shows the priority of logic to those sciences.

Once again, consider ethics which is the science of correct action as opposed to correct reasoning. All human action is being but not all being is human action. So, since being and what belongs to being as being are included in human action but not *vice versa*, then ethics is narrower and less basic than metaphysics. And yet, as a branch of philosophy and as a practical as opposed to a theoretical science, ethics is wider and more fundamental than any one of the other specialized practical sciences. That is because ethics concerns acting correctly just as a person and not acting correctly as a doctor, a carpenter, a dentist, and so on. Good doctors, carpenters, dentists, etc. might be bad persons. The idea of a person acting correctly enters into the idea of a person acting correctly as a doctor, or as a carpenter, or as a dentist, and so on, but not *vice versa*. Otherwise acting correctly is identified with acting correctly as in one specialized capacity, i.e. as doctor, as carpenter, as dentist, etc. dentist. So the idea of a person acting correctly is logically prior to the idea of a person acting correctly as doctor, carpenter, dentist, etc. Moreover, the idea of a person evidently enters into that of a doctor, carpenter, dentist, etc. but not *vice versa*. Otherwise all persons are doctors or they are all carpenters, or they are all dentists, etc. So the idea of a person is logically prior to that of a doctor, carpenter, or dentist, and so on. Therefore, ethics or the science that concerns acting correctly just as persons is logically prior to medicine, carpentry, dentistry or any other specialized practical science. It is first or primary practical science whereas all the other practical sciences in relation to it are secondary practical sciences.

Persons act correctly as just as persons when their actions are virtuous. And persons' actions are virtuous just when they accord with their nature as rational as opposed to brute animals. Otherwise their actions contradict their very own natures. Among animals, only humans can act either virtuously or viciously in the moral sense. That is because only humans can choose to act either in accordance with or against their own natures.

In any case, what are these virtuous actions of persons? They are just those that follow right reason or prudence in being just what is called for in any particular moral situation. They do this when they are neither excessive nor defective but just right. Thus, if I can help a number of starving persons with whom I am acquainted, I rationally decide what amount I should give to each one of them, weighing all factors. If I act correctly as a person, then I give just the right amount at the right time and under the right circumstances to each one, neither too much nor too little, if all are to be best served. In short, I strike the golden mean in exemplifying the virtue of charity.

Practitioners in any one of the specialized practical sciences use actions of the same kind to reach the ends of those sciences. Shunning the extremes of both excess and defect, those actions are supposed to be just right, neither too much nor too little. These balanced actions are called actions that accord with right reason. Thus, a doctor who acts correctly as doctor prescribes just the right amount of medicine, rest or exercise for a patient, neither too much nor too little. A carpenter who acts right as carpenter fits a door or window into a frame with just the right amount of clearance, neither too tightly nor too loosely. He cuts the angle of a plank neither too narrowly nor too widely but just right in view of the end. Or a dentist who acts right as a dentist fills a tooth neither too high nor too low, but again just right in view of the end which is the patient's dental well-being.

Here again the priority of the branch of philosophy called ethics to any one of the specialized sciences is shown. The difference is that since ethics is a practical and not a theoretical science, then the priority in question is that of ethics to any one of the specialized *practical* sciences. For the idea of a person's acting in accord with right reason enters into the idea of a person's acting in accord with right reason in medicine, carpentry, dentistry, and so on, but not *vice versa*. And ethics evidently concerns acting according to right reason *period*, just as a person.

BEING AS ESSENCE AND BEING AS EXISTENCE

Philosophy and particularly metaphysics having been defended, and the priority of metaphysics and other branches of philosophy to the specialized sciences having been shown, attention must be focused more narrowly on metaphysics. In particular, the idea of being as being must be spelled out.

Toward that end, consider these two pairs of questions: (A) "What is it for a being to be changeable"? "What is it for a changeable thing to be a being"? and (B) "What is it for a being to be quantified"? "What is it for a quantified thing to be a being"? Though they have the same content, these two questions in (A) and (B) run in different directions and so have a different form. The first one in each pair proceeds from general to specific while the second goes from specific to general. In each set, the goal of the first question is to concretize the abstract, while the goal of the second is to abstract from the concrete. In (A), the first question begins with any being like a stone or a toad and asks not what it is for it to be a stone or a tree but what it is for it to be changeable. But the second begins with the same stone or tree and asks not what it is for it to be a stone or a tree or changeable, but rather, more broadly, what it is for it to be a being. The stone or the tree is thus a complex of what makes it i) a stone or tree, ii) a changeable thing, and iii) a being. Since it is possible that there are unchangeable things (say, numbers) it is possible that something includes the principles of being but not the principles of change. That shows why metaphysics is about everything and why its principles (such as essence and existence) are included in everything, whereas natural philosophy, which deals with changeable being, is neither about everything nor are its principles, form and matter, necessarily included in everything. In (B), the first question again begins with any being like a stone or a tree and asks what it is for it to be quantified. But the second starts with the same stone or tree — this time considered not as changeable but as quantified — and asks, more broadly, what it is for that stone or tree to be a being. The stone or tree is thus taken as a complex, this time of what makes it a quantified being and what makes it a being. And since it is possible that there is something that is not quantified, it is possible that something includes the principles of being but not either the principles of quantity or the principles of change.

For example, the idea *tree* includes the idea *plant* plus some difference, and the idea *plant* includes the idea *organism* plus some difference, and the idea *organism* in turn includes the idea *substance* plus some difference. In the same way, to the extent that it is changeable, any particular tree includes the principles of changeable being. But a changeable thing includes the principles of quantified being, and a quantified being includes the principles of being as such. Therefore, any particular tree includes the principles of all three, just as the idea of *tree* includes every genus above it. This conceptual hierarchy again shows why metaphysics is about everything and why its principles — but not necessarily the principles of any other science — are included in every being. It also shows what the expression "being taken just as being" means. Third, it shows why metaphysics, to the extent that it deals with just being, is prior to every other science, including the philosophy of nature, which considers being as changeable, and mathematics which considers being as quantified. For, for concepts F, G, and H, if H includes both F and G, if G includes F, and if F includes no other concept, then not only are G and H logically posterior to F, but F is logically speaking the very first concept. Any science that deals with just F, then, is the absolutely first science.

Yet this logically first concept, being, is not the widest genus. That is because it is not a genus at all. Genus and difference being correlative terms, there must be a difference if there is a genus. Yet, since there is nothing outside of being from which any difference can come, it follows that being is not a genus and hence not the widest genus. Nor can it be said that this simplest and most primitive concept of being is either a species or a difference. Any species is by definition composed of genus and difference and so is composite. But the idea of being as such is utterly simple. And any difference marks off one species of a genus from others. But it is evidently not by being that one species differs from another. If two or more species or individuals differ, they evidently do not differ by that by which they are alike.

Being is not a genus, species, or difference because being is not to begin with an univocal term. Genus is said univocally of its species, as, for example, animal is said univocally of tiger, bear, and fox. Species is said univocally of its member individuals, as, for example, human is said univocally of Socrates, Plato and Aristotle. And difference is said univocally of the individuals who belong to the species, as, for example, rational is said univocally of these same philosophers. However, in its fundamental sense of *esse* or act of existing, being does not apply univocally to two or more individuals. True, my act of existence is related to my human essence as a stone's or a tree's or a cat's act of existence is related to a stone's or a tree's or a cat's essence. But in each case, the act of existence is unique and unrepeatable.

Another way of putting this is to review Kant's argument to show that to be or to exist is not a predicate.[5] And of course, if existence is not a predicate to begin with, then it cannot be predicated univocally of many and so cannot be either a genus, species, difference, or any one of the other other predicables. If being in the sense of existence is assumed to be a predicate, says Kant, then there would be a difference *in concept* between a hundred real dollars and a hundred imaginary dollars. But the two are not different in concept. By contrast, the concept of a hundred dollars and the concept of ninety dollars *are* different in concept. It follows that existence is not a predicate and hence is neither predicable of many nor identified with any one of the predicables of logic. Besides, says Kant, if being or existence is a predicate, then our concepts never correspond to reality. For the object of any one of our concepts then has a property (i.e. real or extra-mental being or existence) which the concept lacks. So, since our concepts then always fall short of their objects — the latter having a property which the former lacks — universal skepticism is installed. So unless one countenances universal skepticism, being or existence is not a predicate and hence neither univocally predicated of many nor identified with any one of the predicables.

Nevertheless, in addition to meaning existence, 'being' sometimes means essence. We signify essence as over against existence in ordinary language just when we ask what something is as opposed to asking whether it is. When we do, we want to know what its essence is. For that reason and in contrast to being in the sense of existence, being in the sense of essence is equivalent to the species. That is because being in the sense of essence is what the definition of something signifies, and species is what the definition signifies. Thus, essence is expressed by the phrase "_ is an F" as when it is said that Fido is a dog or that Felix is a cat, or that Socrates is human, and so on. Moreover, while essence refers primarily to species, essence refers in a secondary sense to accidents. Thus, to the extent that "_ is wise," "_ is six feet tall," "_ is running," "_ is the teacher of," etc. also signify what something is (albeit accidentally), these and other such phrases also signify essence. But something has essence the way it has existence and accidents necessarily exist in a species whereas no species exists in an accident. A sign of this is that accidents are predicable of species but not *vice versa*. For example, we say that a fox is running but it is nonsense to say that running is a fox. Thus, species are independent of accidents in a way that accidents are not independent of species. It follows that though accidents are being in the sense of essence, they are so in a derived, secondary sense of essence.

However, it is wrong to think that being primarily means essence even when essence is taken in the primary sense of species. For being a human, being a fox, being a tree, etc. all of them express being in the sense of possibility, and the actual or the existent is prior to the possible. That is what is behind the dictum that existence precedes essence. To see this tie between essence and possibility, take the idea of an endangered species, say a condor. Though most of us have a vague notion of the bird, ornithologists have a precise idea of it. They know further details about it. Now suppose the existential status of condors is so grave that, for all anyone knows, the last condor expired last night on a cliff in the Andes Mountains. Then while ornithologists can answer the question, "*What are* condors"?, they do not know that *there are* condors. And they would be the first to admit their doubt. That shows that essence is not existence.[6] So even though the essence or "what" of a condor is form and act with respect to the condor's matter of which that same condor essence is the form or act, that same essence is potential or possible with respect to any condor's individual act of existence.

Alternatively, essence is what the definition of a thing signifies. But the definition of a thing is equivalent to its species. So the essence of a thing is what its species signifies. Yet to be or to exist is not what a thing's species signifies. Otherwise to know the species of a thing is to know that it exists.

But this is false as is shown by the case of condors. It follows that the essence of a thing is distinct from its existence.

Moreover, saying that existence actualizes essence means that essence as such is a possible. Aquinas's example is that of a phoenix.[7] We believe that a phoenix is only a mythical bird. But we nonetheless know what it is. We can describe it in some detail. Yet we say that it is only a possibility. There could be phoenixes but actually there are not. But just in case a real phoenix shows up, that possibility is actualized. Only then do we say that there are phoenixes. That implies that, taken just in itself and as such, essence is being in the sense of a possible.

Existence, then, is logically prior to essence because the actual is logically prior to the possible. To exist just signifies the actualizing of what is possible, whatever that possible thing might be. Moreover, existence is the good or perfection of essence, according to Aquinas. For following Aristotle, Aquinas holds that the actual is the end or goal of the potential and the end or goal of a thing is its good or perfection. So existence is the good and perfection of essence.[8] Under this line of argument, then, essence has a bent toward its good or fulfillment and that is its existence.

Finally, it can be said that at least in creatures, essence and existence are not only distinct but interdependent. Language reflects this interdependence. Suppose that I spy a herd of animals in the distance and say, "There *are*....." The reaction of my companions is to ask, "*What* are there"? In other words, existence-claims that lack a property or essence symbol are incomplete. The same goes for predicates without a symbol for a subject. They are incomplete the way logical functions like 'Fxy' are incomplete. Suppose that A overhears B to say, "....is tall." A's reaction is, "*Who* is tall"? As in language there are no statements to the effect that something exists without a sign for some essence or other, so also are there in language no statements of something's having a predicate without a sign for an existent subject. It is clear that the reason for this is the reciprocity of essence and existence in the facts which these true statements are about.

Stated differently, between essence and existence is a reciprocity. Existence actualizes essence but in so doing existence does not compromise the integrity of essence. It adds no property to it that in its possible state essence lacks. To say otherwise repeats the mistake of rationalist philosophers like Descartes, Spinoza and St. Anselm. At the same time, essence determines the level of existence. How persons exist is evidently higher than how sticks and stones exist.

Here, one finds an epistemological analogy. This is the interdependence of consciousness and the object of consciousness. Any thing whatever is a possible object of consciousness. It becomes an actual such object only when someone is conscious of it. There might be a stone on the floor but only when someone sees or thinks about that stone does it become an actual object of consciousness. Thus, any object of consciousness is to the consciousness of it as essence is to existence. As the act of consciousness makes any object *be* an object of consciousness, so existence makes any essence *be* that essence. Yet the level of any awareness or consciousness varies with the level of its object. Not just the object thought about but even the thinking of it is elevated when I go from being aware of a stone to being aware of a person. The culmination of this according to Aquinas occurs when one knows God in the Beatific Vision. Since God is the highest object of knowledge, the corresponding act of knowing achieves its highest possible notch.[9] Knowing God in the Beatific Vision is immeasurably higher than knowing any creature because God is creator and not creature. So, just as the higher an object of knowledge is the higher is the knowing of it, so too the higher any essence is relative to another, the higher the existence of that essence is to the existence of the other.

Finally, it can be said that Thomistic existentialism avoids both the false absolutization of essence and the false absolutization of existence. The first is the error of essentialism or rationalism. The second is the error of irrationalism. Paradoxically, when you stress essence to the detriment of existence you wind up denigrating essence. And paradoxically again, when you stress existence to the demise of essence you end up undermining existence. That is because essence and existence are interdependent.

To spell it out, when essence swallows existence it is essence itself that is destroyed. Aggrandizing essence spells the demise of essence. For suppose that a thing's existence is construed as being a property of it. Then, since that real existence is not a property of that essence as known by us in a concept (since, otherwise, the real thing is in my mind), then it follows that essence as known by us is always devoid of some property that it has in reality. But in that case, Kant's point takes hold. None of our ideas or concepts conform to the world. Since we never grasp essences by our concepts, therefore, the former forever elude us. But essence is nothing if it is not knowable. So the error and irony of all rationalist philosophers is that, bent on maximizing intelligibility, they so extend essence beyond its boundaries that it absorbs existence. And then all intelligibility is lost. To the extent that essence is made to absorb or include existence it to that same extent loses intelligibility and so ceases to be essence.

Eschewing rationalism, some modern existentialists make the opposite error. They fail to see that aggrandizing existence to the detriment of essence only backfires on existence itself. But this only undermines their existentialism. To spell it out, recall Sartre's view that existence never turns on essence. Persons do not choose and act the way they do due to some static, *a priori* essence that they exemplify and which is either in a platonic heaven or in God's mind. Otherwise, free choice having been obliterated, there is no human risk or dread. It makes sense to refer to essence only if essence is the result of and not the precondition of existence. Only after a person shows up in the world and makes choices does he or she acquire an essence, says Sartre.[10] I might choose with good or bad faith but in neither case is it from some preexisting essence that such choice issues. Otherwise existence follows on essence and free choice is destroyed. This Sartrean existentialist stance is just the opposite of essentialism. Instead of it being the case that essence absorbs existence, existence stamps out essence. If under classical rationalism a person is only essence, under Sartrean existentialism a person is only existence.

But when existence thus blots out essence, it is existence itself that collapses. In this, Sartrean existentialism is no less self-destructive than the static essentialism it opposes. If persons are existence without essence, then human existence or subjectivity, the core of at least Sartrean existentialism, unravels. If one's existence is not through one's essence, then one's projecting oneself into the future by free choice and action does not issue from the *kind* of thing a person is but from his or her existence. And then, non-persons do not exist. They only have being. But then the perplexing consequence of this is that *there are* things (i.e. non-persons) that do *not* exist. This avoids inconsistency only if the operator "there are" is not an *existential* operator after all but a sign that that over which it ranges somehow has being but not existence. But then in saying, "There are persons in the pool," existentialists cannot mean that these persons *exist*. But if to exist is to be a person or to have subjectivity, then in saying, "There are persons in the pool" existentialists say that these persons do *not* exist or have subjectivity. The only way to skirt this is to hold that "there are" sometimes functions as an existential operator and sometimes not, depending on what it ranges over. But the capriciousness of this aside, how do existentialists of this sort consistently say that whether "there are" signifies *existence* or not turns on the *kind* of thing to which that expression refers? For that is to concede what no existentialist countenances, namely, that whether or not one can say of something that it exists is settled or determined by that thing's essence.

Put differently, to say that persons exist but that non-persons do not exist but only have being implies that the one who says this holds that persons and non-persons are different *kinds* of thing. No one says that there are penguins but not phoenixes unless he or she believes that they are birds of a different kind. But no sooner does one allow a difference in kind between persons and non-persons than one implies that persons are not just existence but a mix of existence and essence. For a thing's essence is just the kind of thing that it is.

NOTES

1. This is controversial since some hold that truth is independent of minds. A defense of the mind-dependent status of truth is presented in Chapter Four. Here it must suffice to say that truth is where falsehood is, and that falsehood is not in things but in minds.

2. See Aristotle, *Nicomachean Ethics* trans. Terence Irwin (Indianapolis: Hackett Publishing Co., 1985), Book II, 1103b, 26–28, 35.

3. Aristotle, *Physics*, trans. R. Hardie and R. Gaye in R. McKeon, ed., *The Basic Works of Aristotle* (New York: Random House, 1941) Book I, Chapter seven, 190a-191a, 230–233.

4. C.S. Peirce, "How to Make Our Ideas Clear" in M. Fisch, ed., *Classic American Philosophers* (Englewood Cliffs, N.J.: Prentice-Hall, Inc., 1951), 77–80.

5. Kant, *Critique of Pure Reason*, trans. N. Kemp Smith (London: MacMillan &Co., 1958) B626–B628, 504–506.

6. St. Thomas Aquinas, *On Being and Essence*, trans. by A. Maurer, (Toronto: Pontifical Institute of Medieval Studies, 1949), Chapter IV, 46.

7. Ibid.

8. St. Thomas Aquinas, *On Truth*, trans. R.W. Schmidt (Indianapolis: Hackett Publishing Co., 1994), vol. III, q. XXI, a. 2.

9. St. Thomas Aquinas, *Summa contra gentiles*, in A. Pegis, trans., *Introduction to St. Thomas Aquinas* (New York: The Modern Library, 1948), Book III, Chapter XXV, 442–447.

10. Jean-Paul Sartre, *Existentialism and Human Emotions*, (New York: Philosophical Library, 1957), 12–18.

Chapter Two

God

Besides answering some stock objections to metaphysics, Chapter One sought to show A) the logical priority of philosophy to the specialized sciences, B) the priority of the idea of being to that of any other concept, and C) as within the idea of being, the priority of existence to essence. As to B), every other concept adds to being some aspect which is not included in being. Instead, being is included in them. The idea of being is evidently included in the idea of quantified being but not *vice versa*; and the idea of being is also included in the idea of changeable being but again not *vice versa*. That shows the priority of metaphysics to both the other speculative sciences like mathematics and philosophy of nature and to any and every empirical science. As to C), if the actual is logically prior to the possible or the potential, then 'is' or 'being' in the sense of existence is prior to 'is' or 'being' in the sense of essence. For existence is to essence as the actual is to the possible or potential. This is reflected in language which signifies being in the sense of existence by a verb, i.e. 'exists' or 'are.' Thus we say that there *are* condors or that condors *exist*, where the 'are' and 'exist' denote actuality. By contrast, no verb corresponds to being in the sense of essence.

That aside, let us focus on being in this same sense of to be or to exist. Here, Aquinas not only distinguishes 'exists substantially' from 'exists accidentally,' but he also distinguishes 'exists contingently' from 'exists necessarily.' The first divides an apple, say, from its red color or round shape. The apple in my hand exists substantially in the sense that it does not exist in something the way in which its color or shape exists in it. True, the apple exists in my hand, but this is a different sense of 'in' than the sense of 'in' that is meant when we say that the apple's red color or its round shape exists in the apple. What is meant by the latter sense of 'in' is that the color and shape are incapable of existing apart from the apple or at least apart from something or other. For that reason, we say that the apple is a thing or a substance whereas its color and shape are accidents.

The second distinction divides substances into those that are generable and corruptible and those that are ingenerable and incorruptible. Aquinas calls the former possible beings (since they can either be or not be) and the latter necessary beings.[1] Thus, apples are generable and corruptible and hence contingent beings. But all separated substances such as angels and God in the view of Aquinas are ingenerable and incorruptible and so are necessary beings. So in his view are primary matter and human souls. In any case, just as a certain shape or color exists only because some body exists of which it is the shape or color, so too any possible being exists only because a necessary being exists.[2] Each case involves total dependency though in different ways. Shape is an accident and accidents depend on the substance of which they are the accidents. By this it is meant that the idea of substance enters into the definition of accident. You cannot define shape or for that matter any other accident *taken as accident* without bringing in the idea of substance. A body, on the other and, is a substance in its own right and not an accident. It does not, therefore, *qua* substance, depend on substance internally, i.e. in that substance enters into its definition. If nothing else, that would be circular. Still, a body does depend on substance externally, if not internally. By this it is meant that ultimately any body, according to Aquinas, depends on another substance, an uncaused being, as the continuous cause of its being or existence. Unless an uncaused being exists, no body exists.

This follows from the fact that bodies are generable and corruptible and hence caused beings. As such, bodies in the long run depend on an uncaused being to be. A caused being is one that is not identified with its own existence. Otherwise its essence would be to be and thus it would not be a caused being after all but an uncaused being. Here, two propositions must be shown. First, that bodies are caused beings, and second that, to be, such beings depend on an uncaused being.

That bodies are caused beings follows from the fact that they are not identified with their essences. If something x is identified with its own existence so that x's essence is one with its existence, then x is *ipso facto* identified with its essence.[3] Otherwise, there being more to x than its essence, there is more to x than its existence. And then it is untrue to say in the first place that x is identified with its existence. But bodies are evidently not identified with their own essences. It follows that bodies are not identified with their own acts of existence and so are caused beings. In behalf of the second premise, take this dog Fido. Fido is not identified with dogness. Otherwise to be dog is to be Fido. And then Fido and Rex are not two dogs but one. Fido, then, is more than his essence dogness. If, though, Fido is one with his act of existence so that his essence and existence are one, then Fido is not more than his essence dogness. It follows that Fido is more than his act of existence. Essence and existence thus being distinct in Fido, it follows that Fido is caused by something else and so is not a self-existent being.

Second, that caused beings like bodies depend on an uncaused being is shown as follows. Whatever is, say a, but is not identical with its own act of existence, is evidently composed of existence plus some essence of which it is the existence. Thus, since Fido is not identified with his act of existence (otherwise Fido always is), then Fido is composed of that individual act of existence together with that of which it is the act, i.e. the essence of being a dog. But if a's existence is distinct from a's essence as two different sides of a, then the former is accidental to the latter. Otherwise to be dog is to be Fido. But if something is accidental to an essence then its presence with or in that essence is due to some external thing. By analogy, if being 100 degrees Fahrenheit is accidental to water, then that some water has that temperature is due to something external to water, say, fire. Therefore, if a is not identified with its own act of existence but is a composite of that act plus some essence, then a's existing, like the heat of the water, is due to something external to a, say, b.

However, if b's existence is distinct from and so accidental to b's essence just as is the case with a's, then b's existence cannot be cited as the explanation of a's. True, if existence is accidental to essence in a (i.e. if a is a contingent being) then existence in a is caused by something else. Yet the latter cannot be something else b in which existence is also accidental to essence. For since what must be explained in a is a's existence, this can hardly be accounted for by something else whose existence, like a's, also requires explanation. Otherwise one explains something in terms of itself, i.e. one explains what is indifferent to either existence or non-existence in terms of what is indifferent to either existence or non-existence. Since, therefore, no *explanatio* is or includes the *explanatum* without circularity, it follows that the only sufficient cause or explanation of a caused being is a self-existent being.

Put a little differently, If b's existence, like a's, is distinct from b's essence, then the former is outside of or accidental to the latter, just as is the case with a. And then once again, b's existence is due to some external thing c, and so on. But if this chain of existential dependency proceeds to infinity, then none of the members of that chain in the first instance exist. b's existence is not a sufficient reason of a's when b's existence is itself simultaneously caused by c's. By analogy, the movement of a cane is not a sufficient reason of the movement of a rock on the ground if the cane moves the rock only because it, the cane, is simultaneously moved by me. Unless, then, there is a being the essence of which is to be, then there is no being like a, b, or Fido whose essence is not to be. If there are things that exist *per accidens*, then there must be something that exists *per se*. Otherwise something that is not its own sufficient reason exists without sufficient reason.

This line of argument can be cast in terms of the idea of existential neutrality or existential indifference. To spell it out, being neutral or indifferent is often unacceptable. We understandably recoil when persons are indifferent either to our own concerns, questions or pain or to that of others. Some years ago a young woman was robbed and assaulted in broad daylight on a street in Manhattan. There was general outrage when it was learned that passers-by did nothing to help her, choosing to remain neutral in her ordeal. Yet neutrality in another sense is praiseworthy. In making calls on players, umpires are expected to be neutral or indifferent to the players' color, race, or team-affiliation.

Besides this personal neutrality, there is impersonal neutrality. Call it existential neutrality or existential indifference. It has two dimensions in each one of which the indifference in question covers data which otherwise go uncovered. That shows its importance for philosophy. The first is the existential neutrality of essence or properties and the datum it covers is judgment. To the extent that logic hangs on judgment which in turn assumes the existential neutrality of properties, it follows that the latter is the ground of logic. That ontology gets behind logic in this way Aquinas stresses in his *On Being and Essence*.[4] His idea that predication requires existential neutrality is just this: that in order to predicate P of S in any one of the forms of judgment or what are known as the five predicables, what P denotes must be taken as indifferent to existence.

One conveniently shows this by a dilemma. Call it the dilemma of judgment. To spell it out, take the judgment by species, "Tony is a tiger." The dilemma is this: The *tiger* that is truly said of Tony exists either particularly or universally. But neither is possible. Particulars are impredicable. And if it is the universal tiger that is predicated of Tony, then Tony is said to be a universal. For if Tony is a tiger and 'tiger' signifies what is universal, then the absurdity follows that Tony is a universal. Yet we do truly say that Tony is a tiger. How is that possible?

Aquinas' celebrated answer is that it is possible just because of the existential indifference or neutrality of essence or property. In the example, it is the existential neutrality of the property or essence of being a tiger. Analogously, suppose that Jones jogs in the morning and golfs in the afternoon. Just as the jogging and the golfing modes are accidental to Jones who is susceptible of either one, so too are particular and universal existential modes accidental or neutral to *tiger* which can take on either one, depending on whether it is *in re* or *in mente*. This neutral core is the objective sense, intension or essence of the predicate 'tiger.'

In any case, if the property of being a tiger were not indifferent to the particular existence it has in Tony, then it could not be said of any other tiger. For to be a tiger would then to be Tony. But in point of fact it is so predicated. And if that same essence of tiger were not indifferent to the kind of universal existence it takes on in mind as a result of being known *via* the universal concept 'tiger,' then it could not be said of any particular tiger, Tony included. For no particular tiger can be said to be universal. Taken in and of itself, therefore, any essence is existentially neutral or indifferent to existence and it is because it is that judgment and hence logic is possible. Behind judgment and hence logic, therefore, is something ontological and that is that essence is indifferent to existence.

This brings us to the second dimension of existential neutrality. For it is not just Tony's essence, but it is Tony himself who is indifferent or neutral to existence. And as it is with Tony, so is it with every other material thing. Otherwise no account is given of another datum. This time, though, the datum is not the fact of judgment or of our knowing or saying what things like Tony are. It is instead the fact of Tony's existence as a corruptible thing. For suppose on the one hand that Tony is not neutral or indifferent to being. Instead, suppose that being is essential to him so that he necessarily exists. In that case, Tony could not not-be. But it is a fact or datum that Tony is a corruptible thing and hence can cease to be. Therefore, when it concerns existence, Tony is entirely neutral or indifferent. Since he does in fact exist, then it is possible that he exists. The actual implies the possible. And since he is a corruptible thing and will some day cease to exist, then it is also possible that Tony not exist. Here, it is important to see that it is not being said that it is possible that Tony exists and that it is not possible that Tony exists. That is contradictory. Rather is it being said that it is possible that Tony exists (since he actually does exist) and that it is possible that Tony not-exist, and that is a different claim.

Alternatively, suppose on the other hand that Tony is not neutral or indifferent to non-being since it is either physically or logically impossible for Tony to exist. For example, neither centaurs nor round squares are neutral or indifferent to non-being since the former cannot physically exist while the latter cannot even logically exist. However, if that is how it is with Tony, then it is evident that Tony would not exist. But in fact Tony does exist. Therefore, just as the logical datum of our judging that Tony is a tiger implies that Tony's essence of 'being a tiger' is existentially neutral, so too the ontological datum of Tony's existence as a corruptible being implies that Tony himself is existentially neutral.

What, if anything, follows from this? Philosophers have noted that you cannot move from the existence of one thing to that of another, and that certainly holds for existentially neutral things like ourselves and Tony. It hardly follows that there is a bird (or anything else) in the bush because there is a bird in my hand. Nor does it even follow that there is a bush. Yet, after having shown in chapters two and three of his *On Being and Essence* how judgment and hence logic requires the existential neutrality of predicates, Aquinas goes on in chapter four to show how the existential neutrality not of predicates or essences but of things like ourselves or Tony requires something that, so far from being neutral or indifferent to being, is necessarily existent.[5] Unlike Tony or ourselves, it exists *per se* and not *per accidens*. His point is not that we can move from one existentially neutral thing to another until at last we must reach a temporally first necessarily existent thing. In fact, he thinks that it cannot be ruled out that such a temporal series of caused existentially neutral things proceeds to infinity. Besides, while he holds that every effect has a cause, he agrees that we cannot move from the being of one existentially neutral thing to that of another. Nor is his point that because each and every existentially neutral thing has a cause, then there must be a cause of the set of all these things, and that this cause, unlike the members of that set, is necessarily existent. A plainer instance of the fallacy of composition it would be difficult to find.

Instead of these distracting irrelevancies and *non-sequiturs*, his point is this: that while one cannot infer the being of one existentially neutral thing from that of another, or a temporally prior necessary being from temporally posterior contingent or existentially neutral things, one can and must infer an ontologically (not temporally) first necessarily existent thing from the existence of even one existentially neutral thing, say, Tony. The reason for this is nothing hidden or esoteric. It follows on the very idea of neutrality, existential or otherwise. A judge is initially neutral between rival parties. What tilts him to one or the other are the facts in the case. Similarly, an umpire is first neutral between calling a runner safe or out. The neutrality is again settled by the facts, i.e. whether the runner or the ball first reaches the base.

In a different way, Tony too is neutral or indifferent. But instead of being indifferent to one party or the other or to a base-runner's being safe or out, Tony is indifferent to being and to not-being. Otherwise, to repeat, Tony either always is or never is. Therefore, something external to Tony accounts for his being, just as, in the case of the judge or the umpire, something external to them accounts for their respective rulings. Yet it is evident that this cause is not one or more other existentially neutral things. No one says that what moves the judge or umpire to one side or the other are *other* neutral judges or umpires. That hardly explains or is a sufficient condition of their decisions.

To this it might be countered that the analogy limps. Under our argument Tony is neutral to existence even when he exists since he might cease to be. But the judge's or umpire's neutrality ends the moment he makes his decision for or against one party or a runner, respectively. However, the answer to this is that the difference makes no difference. For the point of the analogy is just this: that just as the judge's and umpire's distinctive neutrality implies that their rulings are due to something external to themselves and yet not due to one or more other neutral judges or umpires, so too Tony's essential existential neutrality implies that his existence is due to something external to him but yet once again not due to one or more other existentially neutral things.

It follows that though one invalidly concludes i) that another existentially neutral thing is because Tony is, ii) that because one existentially neutral thing is caused by another and that by another, and so on back in time, then there is a temporally first existentially non-neutral thing, and iii) that an existentially non-neutral thing must be posited as the cause of the set of all existentially neutral things because each and every member of that set is caused by another existentially neutral thing — nevertheless and despite all of this — one validly concludes that because an existentially neutral thing like Tony exists then an existentially non-neutral thing also exists as its only sufficient reason. And this, says Aquinas, is what we call God.

Nevertheless, even if this argument shows that something exists *per se* or is a necessarily existent being, can one move from "x is a necessarily existent being" to "x is God or the highest being"? Kant denied that one can.[6] He held that the move is licensed only by the simple converse of "x is a necessary being implies that x is the highest being," namely, "x is the highest being implies that x is a necessary being." But the trouble is, the latter proposition (call it H) on which the ontological proof turns, falsely construes existence as a property of the highest being. For to say that the highest being is a necessary being is to say that the concept of the highest being includes the concept of existence. So, since the proof of God from the contingency of things in the long run feeds on counting existence as a predicate, then it is no more successful than the ontological proof.

How the cosmological proof requires H Kant shows by differentiating two parts of the proof. In the first part, it appears that the proof differs from the ontological proof. For the second premise of this part (I, 2. below), appeals to experience, whereas the ontological proof proceeds from concepts alone. But Kant claims that this difference masks the real dependence of the proof on H which is the nerve of the ontological proof. This is evident from part two of the proof. In any case, here is how Kant says the first part of the proof runs:

I

1. If anything exists, an absolutely necessary being must also exist.
2. Now I, at least, exist.
3. Therefore an absolutely necessary being exists.

So far the proof is incomplete, according to Kant. For I at best shows that there is a necessary being and not that the necessary being is identified with God. The latter is proved only by showing that a necessary being is the highest being. But the trouble is, this final conclusion of the cosmological proof requires H, says Kant, and it is on H that the ontological proof turns. Kant's summary of the second part of the proof leans on the distinction in traditional logic between simple and limited conversion. It runs as follows:

II

1. If every absolutely necessary being is the most real (highest) of all beings, then some most real (highest) being is an absolutely necessary being (by limited conversion).
2. What is true of some most real (highest) being is true of all most real (highest) beings.
3. Hence, if every absolutely necessary being is the most real (highest) being, then any most real (highest) being is an absolutely necessary being (from 1. and 2.).
4. But if "an absolutely necessary being is the most real (highest) being" implies "the most real (highest) being is a necessary being," then "the most real (highest) being is an absolutely necessary being" implies "an absolutely necessary being is the most real (highest) being" (from 3., assuming limited conversion in 1.) and simple conversion).
5. But H, the highest being is a necessary being.
6. Therefore, a necessary being is the highest being (from 4. and 5.).[7]

II, 6. plus I, 3. together complete the cosmological proof since together they imply the final conclusion that there is a highest being or God. At least this is the way any complete cosmological proof must run, according to Kant. But then since that proof depends on H and H is in the view of Kant rendered H' "the concept of the highest being includes the concept of existence," then the cosmological proof feeds on the basic proposition of the ontological proof in which existence is wrongly construed as a property or predicate.

As against this Kantian objection, Aquinas would deny in the first instance that his own version of the cosmological proof proceeds the way Kant says it does in I above. For to begin with since Aquinas held that angels are also necessary beings even though they owe their existence to something else, he does not mean by 'necessary being' one that is uncaused. Instead, he means by 'necessary being' one that is essentially simple (i.e. one whose essence is not composed of form and matter but is form or matter alone) and hence neither generable nor corruptible. For him, necessary beings are opposed to possible ones or ones that are generable and corruptible. This is evident from the "third way" of his celebrated five ways of showing that God exists. So his own version of the cosmological proof from non-necessary beings (i.e. ones that are found to be generated and corrupted) does not proceed along the lines of I but as follows (call it A)

A

1. If there are beings in which essence and existence are distinct, (whether they are necessary or not) then there is a being in which essence and existence are not distinct or whose essence is identified with its "to be" or existence.
2. But there *are* beings in which essence and existence are distinct.
3. Therefore, there is a being in which essence and existence are not distinct but whose essence is identified with its existence and this is God.

Having reasoned in this way, then, Aquinas would have thought it unnecessary to show by II above that the being whose essence is identified with its act of existence is the highest or most perfect being. In other words, he would reply that A above is sufficient to show that God or the most perfect being exists. That makes II above unnecessary for the proof. But it is precisely in II and not in I, according to Kant, that the mistaken assumption that existence is a predicate occurs (i.e. H above). Therefore, if Aquinas is right, it cannot be charged that his own version of the cosmological proof feeds on that mistake.

To spell it out, no sooner does one prove by A that there is a being whose essence is identical with its act of existence than one *ipso facto* proves that that being is the perfect being or God. For essence and existence being distinct in created beings, existence is to essence in such beings as act is to potentiality. Since, however, act is the end and good of potentiality, it follows that any created being is good to the extent that it is act. But since these same created beings are not just act but in them act is received in something else (i.e. potentiality) which is non-act, then such beings are not just good but a composite of good and non-good. They are therefore said not to *be* goodness but to participate in goodness. So to the extent that you and I and every other creature are a mix of act and potentiality, we are all of us a mix of good and non-good. It follows that since the uncreated being is no such mix but is identified with its very own act of existing, then that being, since it just act, is just good or goodness itself. But a being that is none other than goodness itself is a perfect being. It follows that any uncreated being is *ipso facto* a perfect being.

Nor can there be any more than one such being. For suppose that there are two or more beings whose essences are identified with their acts of existence. Then, neither one of them is identified with its essence. Each one is instead a composite of the essence they share plus whatever individuates each one. But a god or perfect being is not composite but simple. Otherwise it depends on its parts and so is not perfect after all since it is dependent. Hence, since, to be perfect, any god must be identical with its essence, it follows that any such being is one. Besides, suppose that there are two or more such beings and hence that each one is a composite of the divine essence they share plus some individuating principle. Then this principle is either identified with each one's act of existence or not. If so, then the two or more supposed perfect beings fail to be uncreated beings after all since in them essence and existence are distinct. But if not, then once again the beings in question turn out to be composite. For if each one's individuating principle is other than its act of existence, then neither one of these supposed gods is simple but is a composite of its existence and whatever it is that serves as its individuating principle. Further, suppose that there is more than one being in which essence and existence are indistinct. Then, there being more than one of them, no one of them is identified with its essence. By analogy, because there is more than one panda, then not one of them, say, Andy, is identified with the essence of panda. Otherwise to be a panda is to be Andy. But now if no such being is identified with its own essence, then there is evidently something in addition to essence in any such being. But by definition, essence and existence are one in such a being. It follows that there is more to such a being than its act of existence. But in that case that being is not identified with its act of existence and so is not uncreated being. Therefore, the supposition is false and there is but one god or self-existent being. In other words, there can be but one being whose essence and existence are one.

Nevertheless, other objections to the cosmological proof have surfaced. The first is that the argument commits the fallacy of composition. Just because each and every contingent being in the world admittedly has a cause, it does not follow that the world as a whole has a cause. That is like arguing that because each and every banana in a bunch weighs six ounces, then the whole bunch weighs six ounces. The second is that from the existence of any one thing the existence of another thing cannot be inferred. Thus, suppose that there is a lion. From that it cannot be inferred that there is a tiger. The third is that the argument at best shows that the uncaused being is identified with the whole of reality and not that it is identified with a transcendent being that creates and sustains all beings whose essences are distinct from their acts of existence. For example, by a similar argument Spinoza might conclude that God exists where by 'God' it is meant reality as a whole. The fourth is that the proof from contingency mistakenly assumes that a cause or causal contributor is or can be an agent. To say that x is the cause of y means that x is the sum total of those conditions that are necessary to produce y, where by 'conditions' it is meant not agents but events or states of affairs in space-time. The fifth is that the argument falsely assumes that the cause of temporal contingent things is a non-temporal necessary thing. However, something x is meaningfully said to be the cause of another thing y only if x is either simultaneous with or before y. Therefore, x is meaningfully said to be the cause of y only if x and y are both of them in time.

It seems that all these objections can be met. The first misconstrues how the aforementioned proof of Aquinas runs. The proof is not that each and every contingent being has a cause and so there is a non-contingent cause of *the whole set* of contingent things. It is that just because any given being exists whose essence is distinct from its existence, then it is necessary to posit a being whose essence is indistinct from its existence. Whatever else is wrong with this argument, it does not commit the fallacy of composition.

Like the first, the second objection thrives on a half truth. To be sure, from the fact that a lion exists it cannot be inferred that a tiger exists. That is because the existence of any caused being cannot be inferred from the existence of another caused being. But from the existence of a caused being Aquinas' proof infers an uncaused being and not another caused being.

The third objection is relevant only if reality as a whole can from the start be conceived of as being uncaused. But that is not the case. Reality as a whole includes, if it is not identified with, the spatial-temporal world or what some call Nature. However, Nature or the whole system of space-time no more implies existence than does some member of it, say, a lion. Like the lion, Nature or the whole system of space-time can be conceived not to exist. Kant thought that it was *psychologically* impossible for us to imagine the absence of space and time. However that may be, it is beside the point. The non-existence of the spatial-temporal realm is not *logically* inconceivable. It follows that the uncaused being cannot in the first instance be identified with the whole of reality and therefore that the third objection is irrelevant.

The fourth objection assumes that the cause of something or what figures in that cause cannot be an agent. Yet this is not only an arbitrary but also a counterintuitive assumption. When Phidias sculptures *Athene*, the actual efficient cause of the coming-to-be of *Athene* is evidently Phidias as sculpturing. Thus an agent, i.e. Phidias, figures in the explanation of *Athene*. True, conditions other than Phidias' sculpturing are necessary to produce the effect. There must be a block of marble which is undergoing a change in shape, and there must be a mental model for the sake of which Phidias works. But for this model to exist, there must be an agent in whom it exists and by whose action the potentiality in the block to assume the shape of *Athene* is actualized.

The fifth objection assumes, following Hume and Kant, that cause and effect are and must be in time. Time is the condition of change and any instance of the causal relation is an instance of change. In Hume's celebrated example, the stick's impacting the billiard ball is the model of the causal relation. As this example is evidently an instance of change and as time is the condition of change,[8] then it follows that time is the condition of causality. Both cause and effect are therefore in time. It is therefore meaningless to say that God or for that matter any other atemporal thing or state is the cause of a temporal thing or state.

But even if it is granted that all change is in time and so that time is the condition of change, does it follow that all causes are changes? Suppose for the sake of argument that there is a Creator. Then there is causality which is not change. Since all change requires an enduring substrate and creation excludes any pre-existing substrate (since creation is not the production of something out of pre-existing matter but the production of something *ex nihilo* or in its entirety) then creation is not change. But since to create is evidently to cause, it follows that if there is a Creator, then Hume and Kant are wrong and time is not necessarily the condition of causation. For they hold that time is the condition of causation only because of their belief that all causes are changes, and the latter is true only if the idea of a creator is denied. But in that case, this fifth objection to a causal argument like Aquinas's rests on a belief (i.e. that all causes are in time) which is true only if atheism is already assumed or that there is no creator. And to assume this is of course to assume that any argument at all for God's existence must fail. If there is no God or Creator, then no one can prove that there is one. Therefore, to the extent that it rests on the dictum that all causes are changes (and hence in time), the fifth objection to Aquinas's argument already presupposes the failure of that argument. Thus does the fifth objection "stack the deck" against that argument. To defeat the argument, the fifth objection must already assume that the argument fails.

The foregoing discussion of a theistic proof along the lines of Aquinas's was occasioned by distinguishing caused and uncaused being, where 'being' is taken in the sense of existence as opposed to essence. What the proof implies is that whereas caused being is received in some distinct thing (essence) as the actual is received in the potential, uncaused being is not received in some distinct thing at all. Otherwise the essence of such a being does not imply its existence and the uncaused thing is a caused thing. So far from it being the case that God's existence is added *to* or is the existence *of* some distinct essence, God's existence and God's essence are one and the same. God's essence is simply His act of existing.

This can be stated differently. For it can be said that while caused beings or beings in which essence and existence are distinct *participate* in or have being, the uncaused being does not participate in or have being but simply is being. An analogy here can be drawn with Platonic Forms as over and against their exemplifications. For Plato, individual humans participate in the Form of Humanity but the Form of Humanity for its part does not participate in Humanity but is instead that in which other things participate. Otherwise there is a further Form of Humanity, say Humanity Number Two in which the first Humanity participates, and so on *ad infinitum*. Unlike the essence human in me and in you, the Form of Humanity is not added to some further thing, i.e. matter in which it is received. That is why it is correctly said that while being human exists participatively in me and in you, being human exists by itself or non-participatively as the Form of Humanity. That is why too the Form of Humanity is called Humanity Itself as opposed to humanity plus something else (i.e. matter) which is informed by it.

Moreover, to say that the uncaused being *is* being as opposed to *having* being implies that it alone is being in the primary sense and that all else that is said to be is said to be in a secondary, derived sense. In relation to the uncaused being, these caused beings are said to be or exist analogous to the way in which a shadow or image is said to be in relation to the thing of which it is the shadow or image. For caused beings depend as much on the uncaused being as shadows or images depend on their prototypes. Remove a thing and its shadow on a wall or its image in a glass or pool is also removed. Remove God (*per impossibile*) and all caused beings are also removed or fall into nothingness. True, we say that shadows and images are or exist just as we say that their prototypes are or exist, and when we do say this we do not speak falsely. Yet no one thinks that the sense of 'are' or 'exist' is the same in each case. Nor is it totally different as when we refer to both a writing instrument and an enclosure for pigs as a pen. Instead, shadows and images are said to be in a derived or secondary sense. Because they are or exist only because their prototypes are or exist, so they are said to be or exist only in a secondary, derived sense of the term. Linguistic sense here simply reflects reality. It is the same with caused beings. Because they are or exist only because their cause, the uncaused being, exists, so they are said to be or exist only in a secondary, extended sense of 'be' or 'exist.' In both cases 'are' or 'being' is said of the two contrasting things neither univocally nor purely equivocally but rather analogously.

Now as it is with being in the sense of existence, so is it with being in the sense of essence or form. As existence is primarily said of the uncaused being and secondarily said of caused beings, so too, essence or form is primarily said of the former and secondarily said of the latter. This is shown in two steps. First, if God is identified with his existence, then God is also identified with His essence. For if God is not identified with his essence but participates in it (as, say, Socrates participates in the essence human) then there is more to God than his essence, just as there is more to Socrates than his essence. As Socrates is composed of the essence he participates in and some matter which participates in it, so God (if He is *not* identified with His essence) is composed of his essence plus what participates in it. However, essence and existence being one in God, that means that God is a composite of His essence (i.e. His act of existing) together with what participates in that essence. That not only compromises the simplicity of God but it also implies that, like creatures, God is a composite of actuality and potentiality. For what participates is related to that in which it participates as potentiality is related to actuality.

Second, if God does not participate in His essence but simply is His essence, and if the latter simply is His act of existing, then it follows that essence is found in God in a more perfect way than essence is found in Socrates or in any other thing that is unidentified with its essence. For for one thing, essence in creatures such as Socrates is in potentiality to existence. However, since it is one with His act of existing, essence in God is in no way potential but purely actual, and actuality is prior to potentiality. For another, to the extent that essence in creatures like Socrates is always something that is participated in by matter or potentiality, then essence or form as found in creatures is always mixed with matter or potentiality, whereas essence or form in God is unmixed with any matter or potentiality. On the contrary, God is nothing but actuality.

Stated differently, essence is found participatively in creatures or caused things and non-participatively in God, the uncaused being. This just means that in the former essence is received in or the actuation of some potentiality whereas in the latter essence is not received in or the actuation of potentiality but is act alone. Otherwise God is a mix of actuality and potentiality and hence both composite and dependent. It follows that, like existence, essence is found in God in a prior sense and in creatures in a secondary sense. For in the order of existence, essence in creatures is potential with respect to some distinct existence which actualizes that potential, whereas essence in God is not potential with respect to some distinct existence which actuates it but is instead identical with that act of existence. And in the order of essence and among creatures in nature, essence taken this time as act is always found as participated in by matter or spatial-temporal potentiality, whereas essence in God is act pure and simple and not act as participated in by such potentiality. Whether, therefore, it has the sense of existence or the sense of essence, 'being' is said primarily of God, the uncaused being, and secondarily of creatures or caused beings.

Thus are human beings along with all other caused beings fundamentally effects of something else (God). And the latter is in no way an effect but only cause. But since cause is logically prior to effect, it follows that human beings as well as all other caused beings are beings in an ontologically secondary sense of the term. True, all these beings exist and, what is more, their existence is a condition of every property they have. Yet in each case their existence hangs on another, and that is why they are all of them secondary beings in the order of existence. Moreover, all spatial-temporal beings have some nature or essence which is signified by their respective definitions. Yet, since each one of them is one among many members of the same species, they are none of them identified with their own essences but instead participate in their essences. They are to that extent and in the order of essence a composite of essence (form) and some matter which participates in that essence (form). They therefore have a composite and not a simple essence. But since every composite depends on its parts or elements, it follows that these same beings are dependent in the order of essence just as they are dependent in the order of existence. Moreover, every essence of a caused being is potential with respect to its act of existence and potentiality, as was said, is logically posterior to actuality. But being one with the divine act of existing, essence in God or the uncaused being is purely actual. Therefore, just as they have existence in a secondary sense so do all caused things have essence in a secondary sense.

And so it is that spatial-temporal beings are composite in a two-fold sense, i.e. both in the order of existence and in the order of essence. First, being caused beings, they are composed of existence and essence as distinct elements related as actuality to potentiality. This is metaphysical composition in the order of existence. Second, the fact that they are unidentified with their own essences shows that each one of them is composed of essence or form together with matter which participates in and contracts that essence or form. And this is ontological composition in the order of essence. These natural beings are changeable both substantially and accidentally, and Aquinas follows Aristotle in distinguishing four causes of change. Any change in the world has a material, a formal, an efficient and a final cause, the last being the end or goal for the sake of which the agent or efficient cause acts. Moreover, both philosophers consider the final cause to be prior among causes, to be "the cause of causes."[9] Thus for both Aristotle and Aquinas purpose looms large in the world. And it is to this controversial topic of purpose or teleology that we next turn.

NOTES

1. St. Thomas Aquinas, *Summa theologica* in A. Pegis, trans., *Introduction to St. Thomas Aquinas* (New York: The Modern Library, 1948), I, q. 2, a. 3, 26.

2. Aquinas argues for this in his third argument for God's existence in his *Summa theologica* I, q. 2, a. 3, 26.

3. However, the converse does not hold. If in the order of essence something is its own essence — so that there is in x no distinction of essence and supposit — it does not follow that x is one with its act of existence.

4. St. Thomas Aquinas, *On Being and Essence*, trans. A. Maurer, (Toronto: Pontifical Institute of Medieval Studies, 1949) Chapter III, 39–42.

5. Ibid., *On Being and Essence*, Chapter IV, 46–47.

6. Immanuel Kant, *Critique of Pure Reason*, trans. Norman Kemp Smith, (London: MacMillan & Co. LTD., 1958), 508–11.

7. Ibid., *Critique of Pure Reason*, 510–11.

8. Not all philosophers hold that time is the condition of change. Leibniz, for example, held that our idea of time is derived from temporal relations and that the latter are appearances that are derived from the reality of change.

9. See St. Thomas Aquinas, *Summa theologica*, in A. Pegis, trans., I, q. 5, a. 2, reply obj. 1, 36–38. Aristotle too refers to the final cause as being the first cause or mover in nature or the realm of movable things. See Aristotle, *Metaphysics,* trans. W. D. Ross, in R. McKeon, ed., *The*

Basic Works of Aristotle (New York: Random House, 1941) Book K, Chapter 1, 1059a, 38, 851.

Chapter Three

Teleology

Does change imply a final cause which is the end or purpose for which the change occurs? While this might be true when the efficient cause is a person, it has been widely denied in so-called natural changes i.e. in changes in nature that occur independently of human beings. True, *I* act for an end in exercising, i.e. for the sake of health. But do animal and plant activities occur for the sake of an end? And do events in inanimate things have goals toward which they aim? Apart from our own purposes, is there purpose in nature? Generally speaking and roughly from the time of Galileo, philosophers have answered this question in the negative. Explaining natural events and things in terms of some goal at which they aim came to be regarded as a case of anthropocentrism, i.e. of foisting onto nature and natural events and activities the strictly human category of purpose. Yet as was stated at the close of the last chapter, Aristotle and Aquinas not only count purpose as one of the four causes in nature but they also regard it as the cause of causes. If the final cause is the cause of the causality of the efficient cause and for that reason the first mover, and the efficient cause in turn is the cause of matter taking on some form, then the final cause is behind both the efficient and formal causes.

In his *Commentary on Aristotle's Physics*, Aquinas reviews and seemingly accepts five arguments of Aristotle in *Physics* Book II (198b 34-199a 33) in behalf of final causes in nature. Yet most philosophers find these arguments unconvincing.

The first argument is that natural changes take place repeatedly in all or at least in most instances. Yet nothing that happens either in all or most instances happens by chance. It is not just by chance that the grass grows in the spring and summer. But everything whatsoever happens either by chance or for some purpose. Hence, all natural changes occur for some purpose. To this one might reply by questioning the last premise. Why say that the disjunction covers all possibilities? Might not something occur out of physical necessity instead of by chance or for some purpose?

The second argument proceeds as follows. If something is done naturally, then it is disposed to be done and *vice versa*. But things that happen naturally occur such that they lead to an end in the sense of a final result. Therefore, supposing that there are no obstacles, things that happen naturally occur in such a way that they are disposed to be done. But for something to be disposed to be done is for it to be done for the sake of an end or goal. It follows that natural change happens for the sake of some end or goal.

Aquinas supplies an example as regards the second premise. Among trees, first comes the roots, then the trunk, and at last the top-branches. In this temporal ordering art follows nature. In house-construction, first comes the foundation, then the walls, and then the roof. In each one of these cases, one stage follows on another until the end-result is reached.

Yet one might challenge the first premise. Why just because things in fact happen in nature in a certain order, does it follow that they are disposed to happen in that order? Aquinas might reply that the fact that they regularly do occur in a certain order rules out their occurring in that order by chance. However, this does not imply that they are from the start or *a priori* disposed to happen the way they do, i.e. that they happen by purpose or design. Once again, the tacit presupposition of the argument seems to be that things occur in nature either by chance or by design and by no other alternative.

Third, some things are made by art but not by nature and conversely. A house is made by art or craft but not by nature while a tree is made by nature but not by art or craft. But in things that are made both by art and by nature (e.g. health) art copies nature. Art follow nature in healing by heating and cooling. However, things produced by art or craft are produced on purpose. Therefore, things produced by nature are produced on purpose.

Yet even if one supposes that some things are made both by art and by nature and that in such cases art copies nature, the question is whether, in such cases, art *in all respects* mimics nature. This third proof succeeds only if this is assumed true and this assumption goes undefended.

The fourth argument is this. Since some insects and animals always act in the same way, it is evident that they do not act by art, inquiry, or deliberation. For what acts by art, inquiry, or deliberation acts by intelligence. However, what acts by intelligence does not always act in the same way. Not every builder constructs a house in the same way. Yet spiders, bees, ants, birds, etc. always make their homes or nests in the same way. That is why some believe that they do act by intelligence. So, since the activities of insects and animals are evidently for the sake of an end but are not due to intelligence, then they are due to nature. But then it follows that nature acts for goals or purposes.

Nevertheless, let it be assumed both that some insects and animals always act in the same way and that this uniformity precludes their acting from intelligence. From this it scarcely follows that nature itself is telic or acts for purposes. For the possibility remains that this uniformity of action is due to natural necessity and not to purpose.

The fifth and final proof stands on the definition of nature. By 'nature' it is meant either the matter or the form. But the form is the end of change and the nature of an end is that things come to be for its sake. Hence, to be and to come to be for some purpose is found among natural things.

Yet this argument seems to beg the question. If the form that is generated out of matter in any natural change is defined as the end of that generation, then it must be admitted that things in nature occur for the sake of an end or goal. But why should an end in the sense of the end-result of a natural change be identified with an end in the sense of a goal or purpose?

AN ARGUMENT FROM IMMANENT VITAL CHANGES

Nevertheless, a stronger case for natural ends turns on the fact of immanent changes in organisms and the failure of efficient causes alone to cover those changes. This suggests a cause of a different kind, i.e. a final cause. As opposed to transitive changes, immanent changes begin and end in the same thing, i.e. an organism. By contrast, transitive changes begin in one thing and pass over to and end in another. Of this distinction Aquinas writes:

> There are, however, two sorts of operation, as Aristotle teaches in *Metaphysics* IX: one that remains in the agent and is a perfection of it, as the act of sensing, understanding, and willing; another that passes over into an external thing, and is a perfection of the thing made as a result of that operation, the acts of heating, cutting and building, for example.[1]

Aquinas construes a transitive activity as one which begins in one thing and passes over to and produces a change in another thing. It always issues in an effect that is beyond or external to its efficient cause. Thus, a blown tree branch impacts an overhead electric wire, causing it to fall. Or a carpenter begins to build a house. In the former, the motion of the branch passes over to something external to it, namely, the wire, so that the motion is not only in the branch but also in the thing produced by that motion, i.e. the moving wire. In the latter, the act of building in the carpenter passes over to the thing being built, i.e. the house, so that the act of building is both in the carpenter and in the thing being built, i.e. the house. In these cases, something else is being produced besides the activity.[2] In the example of the impacted wire, something else is produced besides the moving branch, namely, motion in the wire. In the example of the house, something else is produced besides the carpenter's building, namely, the house that is being built. As these examples show, transitive changes might be either voluntary or non-voluntary. The blown tree branch is a case of a non-voluntary transitive change while the carpenter's building is an example of a voluntary transitive change. Other examples of the latter are Phidias's cutting *Athene*, DaVinci's painting the *Mona Lisa*, Christopher Wren's building St. Paul's, and so on.

By contrast, an immanent change Aquinas regards as both beginning and ending in the same thing. It does not pass over to and produce a change in some other thing. Unlike transitive operations, immanent operations do not issue in effects that are outside of or external to their agents or efficient causes. They remain in those causes and perfect them. Life is the source of immanent activities all of which proceed from within an organism and are not simply the result of some action on the organism by another thing. All immanent changes occur in living things which, says Aquinas, are self-moved in those changes. Living things have a certain innerness, spontaneity or self-moving power which non-living things lack. By this power all of them grow and assimilate food. Some of them produce eggs and sperm and move from place to place, while others understand, reason, will and choose. Thus,

> Life is essentially that by which a thing is able to move itself, taking the word "movement" in a wide sense, so that even the operation of the intellect can be called "movement." For, those things that can be moved only by an exterior principle are said to be without life.[3]

Yet Aquinas's belief that living things, through their souls, are capable of self-movement occasions two misinterpretations. The first is that the immanent activities through which self-movement is sometimes expressed are entirely independent of external conditions. However, in plants and animals directly, and in us directly as well as sometimes indirectly, these activities depend on material things. Aquinas's idea might be brought out by drawing an analogy to Kant's account of an object of knowledge. Just as the latter for Kant depends on an external thing as well as on the active mind, so too do immanent activities in vegetables, animals and humans depend for Aquinas on external things as well as on the souls of these organisms. Even human rational immanent changes depend to some extent on external conditions. Thus, none of the immanent changes in earthly organisms are purely internal or immanent.[4] Plants receive nourishment through their roots, but the roots in turn depend for this on the condition of the soil. Animals produce living tissue but for this they depend on the food. Since in knowledge humans and brute animals receive the forms of external things that, then knowing, which for Aquinas is an immanent change or activity, is nonetheless dependent on external things.[5] When I sense something, my sensing of it is partly caused by the thing sensed, even though the phantasm or image by which I sense emanates from the soul's power of sense. Further, when I understand what something is, my understanding of it is partly caused by the thing understood, even though the concept by which I understand that thing emanates from the soul's power of abstraction *via* the active intellect.

The second misinterpretation is that Aquinas holds that all self-moved activities or changes are immanent changes or activities. However, from the fact that all immanent changes are in a certain degree self-moved as opposed to being entirely moved by another, it does not follow nor is it the case for him that all self-moved changes are immanent changes. Voluntary activities such as building and sculpturing he clearly counts as examples of transitive activities. Yet the agents in these activities are self-moved to the extent that they act voluntarily in these changes. Phidias is not simultaneously caused to cut *Athene* by a more basic efficient cause which causes him to do so, nor is Wren simultaneously caused to build St. Paul's by a more fundamental efficient cause which pushes his action *a terge*. Otherwise their constructing is not free in the view of Aquinas.

From these distinctions, then, it seems that we can frame the following Thomistic definitions of transitive and immanent activities or changes:

x is a transitive activity in a subject, S =df

(i) x actuates a possibility in s, and

(ii) x does not remain in S but passes over to and causes a change in another thing N.

y is an immanent activity in a subject, S =df

(i) S is the efficient cause of y, and

(ii) y remains in S and does not pass over and cause a change in another thing N.

In any case, to show how in immanent changes final causes must accompany efficient causes, let us consider the immanent change of growth. To spell out the argument, suppose that some growth g occurs in an organism O. Suppose too that g is caused as by an efficient cause by another immanent change in O, and so forth back to the first immanent change (call it f) in O. For its part, is f caused by a previous immanent change in O or is f the effect in a transitive change which begins in some external thing T and ends as f in O?

By an argument which recalls Jonathan Edwards's disproof of Arminian free choice, it can be shown that neither one is the case. Edwards argued that the first free choice of the will is caused either by a preceding free choice in the will or by something outside the will. If the former, then the supposed first free choice of the will is not the first free choice of the will. But if the latter, then the supposed first free choice of the will is caused by something outside the will and hence is not free.[6]

Similarly here, either A), the first immanent change in O, i.e. f, is the effect of another immanent change in O, i.e. $f,$' or B), f is the effect in a change that begins in some external thing T and ends as f in O. However, neither A) nor B) can be admitted. If A) is true, then f, which *ex hypothesi* is the first immanent change in O, is not the first immanent change in O. But if B) is true, then as against the hypothesis once again, f is a transitive and not an immanent change. For then the efficient cause of f is not O but something external to O, say Q, or some change in Q.

Nor can it be said, C), that though f is not the effect *in* a transitive change that begins in S (as efficient cause) and ends in f (effect) nevertheless, f is the effect *of* some transitive change or other that begins in S and ends in O. For example, suppose that a conch bites off some of a sea urchin's spines and that the latter then grows new ones. Let e be the loss of the sea urchin's spines (effect) due to the conch's bite (efficient cause). This is a transitive change which begins in the conch and ends as e in the sea urchin. Further, let g be the subsequent growth of the new spines. Here one cannot say that the transitive change that ends in e is the cause of the immanent change g. True, the sea urchin hardly grows new spines in the places of the old ones unless the latter are destroyed. But that does not mean that the change in which the old ones are destroyed is the *cause* of g. It is clearly only a necessary condition of g. Therefore, one cannot say that though f admittedly is not the effect in a transitive change in which the external thing S is the cause (otherwise f is not an immanent change), nevertheless f is the effect *of* some transitive change or other that begins in S and ends in O. For as the example shows, this confuses a cause with a necessary condition. Therefore, C) above is ruled out no less than are A) and B). It cannot be said that the first immanent change in O, i.e. f, is caused by a transitive change that begins in S and ends in O any more than, in our example, it can be said that the sea urchin's growing new spines is caused by the transitive change in which the old ones are destroyed by the conch's bite. Transitive changes in organisms are at best necessary conditions of, but not causes of, immanent changes in those organisms.

Further, it cannot be countered that the supposed first immanent change in O, i.e. f, is the effect of O taken just as such as opposed to any change, either immanent or transitive. For where the cause is so is the effect. That implies that O engages in f as long as O is O. In other words, O always engages in f. But that contradicts our experience. For example, if it is I taken just as I who am the cause of my own pure and practical reasoning, and if by 'cause' it is meant the sufficient condition of an effect, then so long as I remain the 'I' that I am, I never cease reasoning. Besides, if I am a sufficient condition of any and all my reasoning, then just so long as I remain the 'I' that I am, I engage in all my reasoning at once. But since none of this is admissible, then it cannot be said that O taken as such is the cause of any one of its immanent changes including its first immanent change f. Instead, the actual efficient cause of any change is not any thing taken just as such but taken as specified in some way. Thus, it is not just Phidias but Phidias as sculpturing that is the actual efficient cause of the coming-to-be of *Athene*. Otherwise Phidias always sculptures *Athene* as long as he remains Phidias. And it is not just a paramecium P as such that is the actual efficient cause of its offspring R coming-to-be but P as splitting that is the cause.[7] But the question before us is what causes the causality of this efficient cause? What, in other words, makes P go from potentially splitting to actually splitting?

In addition, it cannot be said that O's nature is the cause of any one of its immanent changes in the sense of being the formal cause of the latter either. For the formal cause of any change is the regular result of the change, and O's form precedes its immanent changes. Thus, when the sun warms a pool of water, the formal cause of the change is simply the warmth which the pool acquires. Generally stated, when anything at all comes to be in a subject S, there is both a "before" and an "after," and the formal cause of the change is nothing but the latter. Thus, the formal cause of P's reproductive changes is R and the formal cause of, say, a tadpole T advancing to a higher growth-stage T+1 is that very stage, i.e. T+1. But as was said, since it precedes rather than follows O's immanent changes, O's form or nature cannot be the formal cause of those changes.

So the question returns: what explains g in O? To answer, some cause c which is not a change, either immanent or transitive, and which is either internal or external to O, explains g. Further, c is not a cause in the sense of an efficient cause, since all such causes are changes, and the latter are either immanent or transitive. Therefore, c is either an immature form of O or the mature form of O taken either as such or as final cause or end of g.

However, c is not an immature form of O, i.e. O as having reached a certain incomplete stage s in its development. For that only calls for a cause of the prior growth, say, g-1, by which O reached s, and so on back to g-n, by which O reached its first developmental stage, say r. So nothing is gained. Nor is c identified with the mature form of O taken as such. Otherwise, since where the cause is so is the effect, then g continues to occur in O even after O reaches its mature form, and this is evidently false. Therefore, it is hypothesized that c is identified with the mature form of O taken as final cause of g.

As final cause or end of g, c both pre-exists g and is like the effect or end-result of g. Yet, c is not internal to O. Otherwise the first horn of the dilemma of ends takes hold. For since c, the mature form of O, in that case already exists in O, then it is contradictory to say that g is tending toward the realization of c. Nothing tends toward what it already is. Therefore, it is hypothesized that c is in a transcendent Mind M in which c functions as the end or final cause of g. By analogy, models pre-exist artifacts that are made after them in artisans' minds as the ends or final causes of those artifacts.

So it is that the cause of g and of every other lower-level immanent change in O is the result or formal cause of that change as it pre-exists in God as end or final cause. Recall that the final cause of a change is specifically the same as that change's formal cause or effect. Thus, those peculiar pre-reproductive changes that occur in our paramecium P are elicited by P's offspring R in God's mind as final cause. Again, those distinctive developmental changes that occur in a tadpole T are drawn out of it by T's more mature form T+1 as it pre-exists in God's mind as final cause, whereas the efficient cause of the change is T as maturing. As to what that maturation, we must conclude (from the previous case of O's growth) that it cannot be a further change, either immanent or transitive. If the former, then to block a regress, a first immanent change in T, say, i, must be posited. But that only reinstates the question. For what then causes i? The answer is the same as before. It can be no previous change, either immanent or transitive. Otherwise either i is not the first immanent change in T or else i is not to begin with an immanent change. The only plausible option, then, is that the cause of T's immanent change of moving to its higher stage T+1 is a cause of a different kind, i.e. a non-change. This can only be a final cause or end which elicits or draws out of T *a fronte* T's moving toward T+1. To do so, it must pre-exist that process *in reason* even though it post-exists or is the end-result of the process *in fact*. By analogy, Phidias's *Athene* is first in his reason even though it is in fact the end-result of his work. It follows that the end or final cause of T's moving from a lower stage to the higher stage T+1 is T+1 itself taken as model or final cause in God's mind. And as it is with T's internal changes, so is it with the internal changes in other lower-level organisms. They are all of them drawn out of those organisms by pre-existing ends. And the latter are just the regular results of those changes as known eternally by God. The difference is that they pre-exist the changes in question as mental or final causes instead of post-existing them as physical or formal causes. Thus do final and formal causes in these changes comprise a unity-in-difference. They are specifically the same but numerically different, each one having a different existential mode, the one ideal and the other real.

Coming to the same conclusion by a step-by-step summary of the previous argument as regards the growth g in O, we get:

1. The growing g is not a transitive but an immanent change. Otherwise g does not end in O but passes over to another thing, T.
2. Nor is g the effect in a transitive change that begins in another thing T and ends as g in O. Otherwise T and not O being the efficient cause of g, g is a transitive and not an immanent change.
3. Nor is g the effect of e where e is itself the effect of a transitive change that begins in T, the efficient cause of e, and ends as e in O. Here, e and not T is the immediate efficient cause of g and T the more remote efficient cause of g. For if T is the efficient cause of e and e is the efficient cause of g, then the external thing T and not O is the efficient

cause of g. But then once again g is a transitive and not an immanent change.
4. So the question is, what explains g in O?
5. Suppose it is said to be a prior immanent change in O, say, g-1, and so on back to the first immanent change in O, say, f.
6. Then in that case, what explains f in O?
7. Not a prior immanent change in O or else f, the supposed first immanent change in O, is not the supposed first immanent change in O.
8. And not a prior transitive change that begins in some external thing T and ends as effect f in O. Otherwise, T and not O being the efficient cause of f, f is not in the first place an immanent change.
9. So the question returns: what explains g in O?
10. To answer, g is explained by some cause c which is not a change, immanent or transitive, and which is either internal or external to O.
11. c is not a cause in the sense of an efficient cause, since all such causes are changes, and the latter are either immanent or transitive.
12. Therefore, c is either an immature form of O or the mature form of O taken either as such or as final cause or end of g.
13. But c is not an immature form of O, i.e. O as having reached a certain incomplete stage s in its development. For that only calls for a cause of the prior growth, say, g-1, by which O reached s, and so on back to g-n, by which O reached its first developmental stage, say r. So nothing is gained.
14. Nor is c the mature form of O taken as such. Otherwise, since where the cause is so is the effect, then g continues to occur in O even after O reaches its mature form, and that is evidently false. Nothing matures after it reaches maturity.
15. Therefore it is hypothesized that c is identified with the mature form of O taken as final cause of g.
16. As final cause or end of g, c pre-exists g. Yet, c is not internal to O. Otherwise, the first horn of the dilemma of ends takes hold. For since c, the mature form of O, already exists in O, then it is contradictory to say that g is tending toward the realization of c.
17. Therefore, it is hypothesized that c is in a transcendent Mind M in which c functions as end or final cause of g. By analogy, models pre-exist artifacts that are made after them in artisans' minds as the ends or final causes of those artifacts.

THE OBJECTION OF INCONSISTENCY

Yet critics will say that saving natural ends in this way only throws out the baby with the bathwater. For if under this view supposed natural ends pre-exist in the mind of God then they are not natural but non-natural ends. But then defenders of natural ends are not defenders of natural ends after all and their view is inconsistent.

To bring out the objection, take an arrow that is flying to its target. To the extent that the end of the arrow is not in it but in the mind of the archer, it lacks a natural end. Its direction to that end is imposed on it by the archer. Similarly, so the objection goes, under our view nothing in or about paramecium P explains the direction of its reproductive changes to their end, R. Since that pre-existing end is not in P but in God's mind, then P, like the arrow, lacks a natural end. Once again, its direction to the end is determined for it by another, in this case by God. The same goes for our tadpole T. Since the end that directs T to its next stage, i.e. T+1, does not actually pre-exist in T but in God's mind, then T's end is not naturally in T. But then like the arrow and P, T too lacks a natural end.

A THOMISTIC REPLY

This is a good objection and it is answered only by refining the concept of a natural end. The idea of a natural end is just the negation of that of a human end to which it is opposed. That means that to say that something has a natural end implies that it neither issues from human choice nor is realized by human action. Otherwise it would be human and not natural purpose, and the corresponding movements or activities would be human and not natural movements or activities. Therefore, all that is required for it to be said that a thing's movements or activities are elicited by a natural end is that those movements or activities are directed to the same non-human made result by the ideal pre-existence of the latter as end. It is not required that that pre-existing end or goal be in matter as opposed to mind. In fact, so far from being necessary for natural ends, this material pre-existence *excludes* natural ends. For it only installs the first horn of the dilemma of final causes. As was stated, if the end already materially exists in the agent, then it is contradictory to say that the latter tends toward it.

Under this definition, then, the analogy of the arrow admittedly limps. Since the arrow's target is made to be its end by human decision or purpose, it is not a natural end of the arrow's flight. By contrast, no human purpose elicits the immanent reproductive and maturing movements in P and T respectively. And yet, since we saw that they are only explained by a final cause, it follows that these movements (unlike the arrow's) are elicited by a natural end.

Even so, the analogy of the arrow, which is Aquinas,' is fitting. For Aquinas' point in using it is to show that just as the ends that things like flying arrows have are given to them by us, so too the ends that natural changes or activities have are given to them by God. The flying arrow has an end only because we have given it one. The means-to-end relation which holds between the arrow's flight and its intended target is imposed onto it by us who have made that physical relation mirror the pre-existing one in our minds. The archer makes the target the end of the arrow which he is about to shoot. Just so, R is the goal of P's reproductive changes only because God has made it so. The relation that holds between P's reproductive changes and R is a means-to-end relation only because and to the extent that it mimics or participates in such a relation in God's mind. Some natural result of an immanent change in the world is called the natural end of that change only because it mimics or exemplifies the Idea of it in God's mind in which that natural result is the end and the change is the means to it. Says Aquinas,

> ...For things which do not know the end do not tend toward the end unless they are directed by one who does know, as the arrow is directed by the archer. Hence, if nature acts for an end, it is necessary that it be ordered by someone who is intelligent. This is the work of providence.[8]

God thus eternally ordains the means-to-end relation between reproducing paramecia and offspring paramecia and therefore that same relation between P's reproductive changes and R. And God eternally installs the means-to-end relation between maturing changes in tadpoles and their next stage of development and hence that same relation between T's maturing and its next stage of development, T+1. The latter along with R are the natural ends of the immanent changes involved only because God makes them so, i.e. only because the pre-existing Ideal models of them in God's mind are the ends of those changes.

Let us spell this out in the case of T's immanent changes. In particular, the result or formal cause of T's moving from a lower to T+1 is the latter, whereas the efficient cause of the change is T as in the process of maturing. As to what in turn triggers that immanent process in T, we saw that it cannot be a further efficient cause either within or outside of T. If the former, then to block a regress, a first immanent change in T, say, C1, must be posited. But that only reinstates the question. For what is the cause of C1? Not any other change, either within or outside of T, as efficient cause of C1. Otherwise, either the first immanent change in T, C1, is not the first immanent change in T or else C1 is not an immanent but a transitive change. The only alternative is that the cause of T's immanent process of moving to T+1 is a cause of a different kind, i.e. a non-change. What can this be but a final cause or end which draws out of *t a fronte* T's moving to the higher stage, T+1? To do this it must pre-exist that process. Moreover, it must be none other than the result or formal cause of the change, namely, T+1. For though an end in change is first in reason, it is last or end-result in existence. As was said, Phidias's

Athene is first in his mind and then the result of his work. It follows that the end or final cause of T's moving from a less developed to the more developed stage T+1 is the Idea of that stage in God's mind.

It is evident that the same analysis applies to P's reproducing R. Here, for the same reasons that were just given, the end or final cause of P's moving from not manifesting to manifesting reproductive activities can only be the Idea of R in God. There, in God's mind, R is just end or end *simpliciter*, whereas in the end-result of the change in the world, R is mixed end, i.e. not just end but end in matter, i.e. end plus this other thing matter in which it is realized. Stated differently, since what participates is related to that in which it participates as matter or potentiality to form, then R as end-result of the change is end participatively speaking whereas R as the preexisting reason or condition of the change in God is end non-participatively speaking. For what participates is related to that in which it participates as matter or potentiality is related to form. From this it follows that in the world and as the result of the change in question, R is truly but secondarily said to be the end of that change, whereas the end of the same change primarily speaking is God. Hence, Aquinas's view that God is the end of all things or that all things desire or tend to God. For him, just as all beings in the world are truly but secondarily called being because they are being as mixed with matter or potentiality and not being *simpliciter* (i.e.being participatively as opposed to being non-participatively), so too, all natural results of immanent change in the world are truly but secondarily called the ends of those changes and not the ends of those changes *simpliciter* or primarily speaking. Instead, God is primarily speaking the (non-participative) end of those changes, just as God is primarily speaking being (or non-participative) being. And it is evident that Aquinas would construe T's immanent change from a less developed stage to T+1 in the very same way.

SUMMARY

So it is that though natural ends are independent of our minds and are for that reason called natural (as opposed to human) ends, they are not independent of God's mind. As divine providential Ideas, they exist *ante rem*, along with the ideas of their means, as so many eternal Ideas of the particular relations that exemplify them *in re*.

From all of this it follows that to the extent that they tend toward their own particular ends, all things tend to God. For as was said, the result of any natural thing's tendency is called the natural end of that thing only because and to the extent that it mimics or participates in what really is the end of that thing's tendency. And that is the Ideal final cause of that result in the mind of God. And this holds for any and all tendencies and ends in the world, whether natural, sensible or intellectual.[9] Moreover, since the end of anything is its good, then all things are good by reason of the divine goodness, i.e. by reason of their participating in some way, however distantly, in the first being or good. Says Aquinas,

> ...Everything is therefore called good from the divine goodness, as from the first exemplary, effective and final principle of all goodness. Nevertheless, everything is called good by reason of the likeness of the divine goodness belonging to it, which is formally its own goodness, whereby it is denominated good. And so of all things there is one goodness, and yet many goodnesses.[10]

NOTES

1. Aquinas, *Summa contra gentiles*, trans. J.F. Anderson (Notre Dame, IN: Univ. of Notre Dame Press, 1975) Book II: Creation, Chapter 1, no. 2., 29.

2. For a clear contrast of transitive and immanent activities on this point, see St. Thomas Aquinas, *Commentary on the Metaphysics of Aristotle*, trans. J.P. Rowan (Chicago: Henry Regnery Co, 1961) vol. II, no. 1862–1864, 688–89.

3. St. Thomas Aquinas, *Commentary on Aristotle's De Anima*, trans. K. Foster, O.P. and S. Humphries, O.P. (New Haven: Yale University Press, 1965), no. 219, 168.

4. Aquinas accords a higher degree of immanence to angels and the highest degree to God. The intelligible species in angels do not depend on extrinsic objects, as they do in us, and unlike either us or angels, God's knowing is not distinct from His being, in which case the intelligible species in God is one with the divine essence. See Aquinas, *Summa contra gentiles*, Book IV, Chapter 11, no. 3–5, 80–81.

5. Ibid., *Summa theologica* trans. A. Pegis, in *Introduction to St. Thomas Aquinas* (New York: The Modern Library, 1948) I, q. 85, a. 1, reply to obj. 3, 404; I, q. 84, a. 2., 380–382.

6. Jonathan Edwards, *Freedom of the Will*, in Faust and Johnson, eds. *Jonathan Edwards* (New York: Hill and Wang, 1962), Part II, section 1, 284–86. Edwards' argument might defeat the Arminian notion of free choice, but whether it works against other notions of free choice (say that of Aquinas) is not evident.

7. Aristotle, *Physics*, in R. McKeon, ed., *The Basic Works of Aristotle*, 195b, 4–6, 242; 195b, 16–21, 242.

8. St. Thomas Aquinas, *Commentary on Aristotle's Physics*, trans. Blackwell, Spath and Thirlkel (New Haven: Yale University Press, 1963) Lecture 12 (198b 10-33) #250, 116.

9. St. Thomas Aquinas, *Summa theologica* trans. A. Pegis, I, q. 44, a. 4, reply to obj. 3, 240–241.

10. Ibid., *Summa theologica* trans. A. Pegis, I, q. 6, a. 4, 50–52.

Chapter Four

Truth, Knowledge and Goodness

TRUTH AND GOODNESS

Truth and goodness do not add anything real to being as, for example, green adds to apple. For whereas green is extrinsic to the definition of apple, nothing real is extrinsic to being. No thing or nature of any sort is outside being taken universally. Nor, apart from adding an accident to being, as does green to apple, do truth and goodness add a difference to being, as rational adds a difference to animal. For difference is outside genus and nothing is outside being.[1] Third, truth and goodness do not add to being some mode or aspect which belongs to one of the ten categories of being. For truth and goodness themselves divide into the ten categories just as being does.[2] That is why scholastic philosophers call them transcendentals. So far from falling under any one of the ten categories, truth and goodness run throughout the categories, thereby transcending any one of them.

Yet, since outside being is nothing, truth and goodness do not add anything real to being. Yet though they add nothing real to being, truth and goodness add some conceptual difference to being which being itself does not express. Being acquires the aspect of truth when it is considered as intelligible, whereas being acquires the aspect of goodness when it is considered as end. Thus, the ideas of truth and goodness imply a relationship to an intellect and to an end, respectively. Truth is being in intellect either as conformed to things or as conformed to by things. In the former case things measure mind while in the latter mind measures things. On the other hand, since good has the nature of an end and the end of anything is its goal and the goal of a thing is its finality or perfection, then the good of something signifies its peak state of being. Thus we say that the mature oak is the good or goal of the sapling, that victory is the good or goal of battle, that happiness is the good or goal of persons as persons, and so on. As truth is being in intellect which either measures or is measured by being, goodness is being as end which always perfects that of which it is the end. Thus Aquinas states that no one correctly defines truth without including intellect in the definition and that no one correctly defines goodness without including the idea of an end in the definition.[3] But since truth and goodness do not add anything real to being but do add the aspect of intelligibility and of end respectively, then this relation is in each case a relation of reason and not a real relation.

As to relations generally, Aquinas follows Aristotle in holding that when a relation depends on its correlative then it is a real relation and *vice versa*.[4] Thus, since desiring depends on the thing desired then desiring is referred to the thing desired as a real relation. It follows that when a relation is not real but one of reason only, then it does not so depend. Thus, since sense depends on the sensible, then sense is referred to the sensible by a real relation. But since the sensible does not depend on sense, then the sensible is referred to sense by a relation of reason. The sensible is called a relation or referable not because it is itself referable but because something else is referred to it, namely, sense. To use Aristotle's examples, "…that which is measurable or knowable or thinkable is called relative because something else involves a reference to it."[5]

Accordingly, since truth and goodness do not add any real relation to being but a relation of reason only, and since what they primarily add to being is the aspect of a measure and an end, respectively, then it follows that their respective correlatives, i.e. the thing measured and that which tends to an end, depend on truth and goodness but that truth and goodness, at least in the primary sense, do not depend on them.

Moreover, though they express different aspects of being, both truth and goodness both express the aspect of perfectiveness. Truth is being in intellect which perfects either intellect or things as the measure of either one. So strictly speaking there is no truth without intellect as subject of truth. Nor is there truth without the aspect which truth adds to being, namely, that of some intellect's measuring or being measured by being.

However, even though it joins truth in expressing being as perfective of something, goodness departs from truth in that it is independent of intellect. Following Aristotle, Aquinas holds that good and evil are in things whereas truth and falsity are in minds.[6] Goodness adds to being the idea of being's perfecting something else as an end. Good is being taken as end which perfects that of which it is the end. Moreover, since end perfects something as the actual perfects the potential, it follows that there is no goodness apart from actual or real being. That is why, following Aristotle, Aquinas denies that there is goodness in mathematics. For the latter deals not with real being and its relations but with logical being or beings of reason. These are numbers, points and the like, all of which for our own purposes and in the science of mathematics we abstract from reality and relate to each other conceptually as so many *entia rationis*. And to repeat, not only is there no goodness without actual being, but there is also no goodness without the aspect which good adds to real being, namely, that of the latter's perfecting something else as its end. But from the fact that mathematical entities are logical and not natural entities, they are abstracted from matter, movement and change. Therefore we explain or prove nothing in mathematics by way of final causes. For example, we say that animals have eyes in order to see, but we do not say that something is the case in mathematics for some end or purpose. Says Aquinas,

> ....we may give as the reason why man has hands that by them he is more capable of executing the things which reason conceives. But in the mathematical sciences no demonstration is made in this way, that something is so because it is better for it to be so, or worse if it were not so; as if one were to say, for example, that the angle in a semi-circle is a right angle because it is better that it be so than be acute or obtuse....[7]

To bring this out, consider the following example, first as regards truth and then as regards goodness. Suppose that I come to know what condors are by closely watching their movements and activities. My (passive) intellect thus moves from knowing condors only potentially to knowing them actually. I become acquainted with the "what" or nature of a condor. Thus is my passive intellect intelligibly specified by the nature or essence of a condor. Since the two correspond, you can say that I have a true idea of a condor and so can make true judgments about them. I truly judge that they nest in the Andes or that they are a bird of prey. Here it can be said that the being in the sense of the essence of a condor is intentionally present in my intellect. Otherwise am I ignorant of condors. But it can also be said that the being that is in my intellect perfects it as a measure perfects what it measures. Something is true, says Aquinas, to the extent that it has the form that is proper to its nature.[8] So intellect is also true in that sense. But since the function of intellect is to know and all knowledge is intentional, then the form that it is proper for intellect to have is the form *of another*. Therefore, being perfects intellect when being is present in intellect, i.e. when the latter's passivity or openness to being in the sense of essence or form is specified or saturated by being in the sense of the essence or form of another. In this case, it is the essence or form of a condor. Yet since in knowledge being is not present in intellect according to its natural existence but instead intentionally and intelligibly, then being in this abstracted state is no more good than the logical entities with which mathematics deals. The mode of perfection whereby being in this logical state in intellect measures intellect adds to being the aspect of true and not that of goodness.

This example illumines what was previously said about how truth adds to being. And that is that truth adds to being the idea of a conformity of being and intellect which makes for the perfection of the latter in the manner of intelligible specificity. What the phrase '...in the manner of intelligible specificity' means is this. Since, to know them, our intellects must receive the species of things intelligibly (i.e. universally and abstractly) and not really (otherwise my intellect becomes a real condor in knowing it), then in knowing species my intellect fulfills its function. That function is to have the species of other things in it intelligibly as opposed to really. Hence, the conformity of being and intellect in which truth consists and in which being fulfills or perfects intellect is a perfection of intellect in the manner of essence or intelligible specificity as opposed to existence. To the extent that being is essence or intelligible specificity it is said to be conformable or assimilated to intellect. For it is essence and not existence that is received in our intellects.

Put differently, having a true idea means that the species, essences or forms of real things (in this case the species, essence or form of a condor) intelligibly specify the passive intellect. But it is just in this intelligible reception of the forms or essences of external things that intellect, so to speak, lives up to itself or has the form or condition that it is proper for its intentional nature to have. Therefore, curiously enough, the human intellect is perfected in its own essence as a cognitive power just when it intentionally becomes something else, i.e. just when it is specified or measured by an external essence. That is what Aquinas means when he says, more formally, that truth adds to being the idea of perfectiveness in the manner of intelligible specificity.[9]

In summary: being as true for Aquinas is being in the sense of essence which is present in some intellect and which measures either that intellect or things in the real world, depending on whether the intellect in question is ours or God's. Truth in our minds (i.e. the universal or essence *post rem*) measures and perfects our minds whereas truth in God's Mind (i.e. the divine Idea or universal *ante rem*) measures and perfects things in the world.

But from a different standpoint, this same example illustrates how good adds to being as well as how truth does. This happens when being is taken not as known or intentionally (as is the case with being as the true) but when being is taken as real being and as perfective of another. To spell it out, the intellect can be taken as a being in its own right as well as something that is known or that is intentionally present in the intellect. In this, intellect is no different from a condor or anything else. It can be considered as it really is or as it is known in intellect. Now we just saw that taken in the latter mode or as known, being in the sense of essence perfects the intellect in the manner of intelligible specificity. That just means that since it is the nature of the intellect to be empty or entirely passive to any and all species or essences (i.e. to be, as it were, "all things" essentially, if intentionally) then any essence as known or as the true perfects the intellect. It gives it essence which in and of itself it lacks and to which it is oriented. So taken as known, intellect too gives intellect essence in the intentional mode, just as does condor as known, tree as known, lion as known, and so on. It is just that what here perfects intellect by being an essence as known by intellect is the essence of intellect itself.

However, taken as a thing or being in its own right and not intentionally or as something known in some intellect, any intellect can move from potentially knowing various essences to actually knowing them. By analogy, condors can move from being mere fledglings or potential adults to being actual adults. The point is that just as their actually becoming adult condors perfects fledgling condors as that to which they are naturally oriented as their end, so too does actually knowing various essences perfect the passive intellect as its end. For it is the nature of the intellect to accord with all things. But since end has the nature of good, it follows that truth or the assimilation of our intellects to things in knowledge constitutes the good of our intellects. Says Aquinas,

> ....nothing prevents truth from being a kind of good insofar as the knowing intellect is taken as a thing. For just as every other thing is said to be good because of its perfection, in a similar fashion the intellect that knows is said to be good because of its truth[10].

This just reflects Aquinas's view that being as good is in things as opposed to being as true which is in the intellect only. It is his view that since in any being two aspects can be considered, i.e. essence and existence, then something can be perfective of another either as regards essence or as regards existence. Being as essence perfects the passive intellect by specifying it or giving it essence in an intentional mode, as was said. So, since the essence that here perfects intellect is essence as known and not essence as existing in nature, this way of perfecting adds the *true* to being. But essence also perfects real things as form perfects matter. Thus the form or essence in any natural thing which is realized in matter, say the form of a horse or a human being, perfects the matter. By analogy, Phidias artistically perfects a slab of marble by imposing onto it the form of *Athene*. In any case, since the essence that here perfects is not essence as known but essence according as it really is, then this way of perfecting adds *good* (and not true) to being. Yet even real essence is perfected by existence as the actual perfects and realizes the potential. For it is our condor's individual and unique act of existence (*esse*) that actuates its essence as a condor. It follows that the act of existence is the good of essence. And since the act of existence is not itself in potentiality to some further act in the world, it is good in a higher sense than essence.

From all this it follows that the true and the good are conceptually reciprocal. In different ways the true falls under the good and the good falls under the true. As a particular good, i.e. the good of the intellect when the latter is taken as thing and not as known, truth falls under good as the particular falls under the universal. Thus Aquinas says that in the order of desirable things, truth stands to good as particular to universal.[11] At the same time, since good is in the intellect as one of its known objects, the good falls under the true as the particular true falls under the universal true. Thus Aquinas states that the order of intelligible things is just the converse of that of desirable things. Instead of the true falling under the good, the good falls under the true. Thus,

> The will and the intellect mutually include one another: for the intellect understands the will, and the will wills the intellect to understand. So then, among the things related to the object of the will, are comprised also those that belong to the intellect; and conversely. Whence, in the order of desirable things, good stands as the universal, and the true as the particular; whereas in the order of intelligible things the converse is the case. From the fact, then, that the true is a kind of good, it follows that the good is prior in the order of desirable things; but not that it is absolutely prior.[12]

THE TWO SIDES OF TRUTH

Truth for Aquinas includes both the truth of judgment and the truth of things. The former might be called logical truth by which it is not meant self-evident truth but propositional truth generally, whether self-evident or not. By contrast, the latter is sometimes called ontological truth by which it is meant that natural things conform to Ideas of them in God's mind. This, with important differences, is the neo-Platonic/Augustinian side of Aquinas's view of truth, whereas his use of 'true' in the sense of the truth of judgments is the Aristotelian side of his idea of truth.

In any case, it is wrong to think that Aquinas identified truth in the proper sense with one of these sides and not the other. Truth is strictly speaking found both in God and in our judgments according to him, the former because things conform to God's intellect and the latter because our intellect conforms to things. The evident difference is that in the former intellect measures things while in the latter things measure intellect. Yet we do predicate 'true' of some things in a derived, improper sense of the term, in his view. For example, the informative use of a spoken sentence might be called true. But it is called true derivatively and improperly speaking. It is called true only because it is a sign of what *is* properly speaking true, i.e. the judgment in the mind of the speaker which the sentence expresses. At the same time he holds that though our judgments are properly speaking true, they are nonetheless secondarily and not primarily speaking true. For their truth is caused or measured by something else, namely, the facts to which they conform. He reserves truth in the primary sense for what owes its truth to nothing else but which is the cause of the truth of all things, and that is God.[13]

In what follows I argue that truth in the proper sense is not confined to judgments or to logical truth in the sense defined. This I do by showing that so far from being derivative of logical truth, ontological truth is the condition of logical truth. Next I show how Aquinas construes the relation of truth to knowledge. This involves degrees of truth the highest of which in us is truth as known.[14] This is that kind of reflective knowledge that occurs when persons are acquainted with the conformity of their own judgments to facts. Second, I show that Aquinas' view implies that in theoretical truth there can be truth without a corresponding knowledge but not *vice versa*. By the same token and in practical truth, it is just the other way around. Here Aquinas' view implies that there can be knowledge without a corresponding truth but not *vice versa*. Finally, I spell out why St. Thomas holds that truth in the proper and primary sense belongs to God alone.

THEORETICAL AND PRACTICAL TRUTH

The idea of being enters into the idea of truth and not conversely. That shows that being is logically prior to truth. No idea is logically prior to being since being is the absolutely first concept.[15] Yet being and truth are the same in extension even if different in intension.[16] That which is true is being and *vice versa*. Being logically posterior to being, truth must add some aspect to being. What does it add? Aquinas' answer is that truth adds to being the idea of a relation to mind.[17] That relation is one of conformity. Truth is being either as conformed to intellect or as conformed to by intellect.[18] It is the agreement of the subjective and the objective, of mind and reality. Alternatively, it is the conformity of something, whether mind or thing, to its source.[19] Yet if truth-bearers are strictly speaking things and not minds, then our judgments are not straightforwardly called true. They are called true only because they are in some way related to things, as for instance, events are called sad only because they make us sad. But our judgments are *themselves* true. They are not called true only because something else to which they are related is true. Besides, if truth is in things and not in minds, then so too is falsehood. But the latter is evidently in minds and not in things. Otherwise what is false is real. But so far from being real, falsehood flouts the real. False judgments are just those that fly in the face of reality.

If truth is strictly speaking in minds, can the terms of the truth-relation be mind-independent? In the case of theoretical truth, which includes both conceptual and judgmental truth, an affirmative answer must be given. When my idea of a condor matches the real condor, the idea is conceptually true. Here the condor is not caused by me or my idea but my idea is caused by the real condor[20]. As for judgmental truth, the fact that condors are birds, to which my judgment to that effect corresponds, does not depend on that judgment. It is accidental to the fact that condors are birds that anyone makes that judgment. Otherwise our true beliefs about the world do not depend on how the world is but how the world is depends on our true beliefs about it. And then the whole meaning of theoretical truth as conformity to reality is lost. So too is the difference between theoretical and practical truth. For in the case of the latter, the things that figure in the truth-relation are necessarily mind-dependent. In practical truth, which covers both productive and moral truth, the thing that enters into the truth-relation *always* depends on minds. If I construct a skiff after my ideal model, the skiff depends on the idea and not the idea on the skiff. The skiff is true because it conforms to my ideal model; my ideal model is not true because it conforms to the skiff. So in productive truth the thing depends on the idea and not *vice versa*.[21] The same goes for moral truth. We say that one's outer or public statements are morally true just when they conform to one's inner or private beliefs. Here, the thing is a statement and the idea it expresses is a belief. And since beliefs are behind statements and not *vice versa*, the thing in moral truth depends on the idea and not the idea on the thing.

From this a further difference follows. Theoretical truth is the conformity of mind to thing whereas practical truth it is the conformity of thing to idea.[22] When I truly judge that condors are birds my belief is made true by things or the corresponding fact. So here in the speculative intellect, ideas are measured or grounded by things. For that reason they are secondarily, if properly speaking true. However, when I build a skiff after my ideal model, it is just the other way around. The skiff is called true just when it matches my idea. Once again, my public statements can be called morally true just when they match my beliefs. So here in the practical intellect, whether productive or moral, things are measured or grounded by ideas and not *vice versa*. It follows that depending on whether it is theoretical or practical; truth is in mind either as measured by things or as the measure or ground of things, respectively.

Yet construing truth as intellect either as measure or as something measured (as do realists like Aquinas, Augustine, Anselm and Scotus)[23], opposes a narrower view of truth. This goes back to Aristotle who as compared to these medieval realists is a minimalist on truth. For him, truth in the strict sense is identified with theoretical truth, which is always measured truth. In particular, truth is found strictly in judgments only and the latter are measured by facts.[24] The same state of affairs which a judgment expresses is found in reality. Thus, "Condors are birds" is true if and only if condors *are* birds. It is only because they bear some relation to a true judgment, therefore, that non-judgments are called true. Thus, ideal models such as my model of the skiff might be called true. But they are so called only in an extended sense. For example, I might elliptically call my model of the skiff true because it is that about which a true judgment can be made, i.e. "This model was behind my skiff." Once again, the skiff is called true not because it really is true but because it gives rise to a true judgment, say, "That is a skiff." And as it is with the model and the skiff, so is it with any other non-judgment that is called true.

Since it both distinguishes various derived senses of 'true' and links them to a single primary sense, this might be called the reductionist view of truth. Under it, 'true' is a *pros hen* equivocal term that applies strictly speaking to judgments and derivatively to everything else. Any derived or extended sense of such a term always includes some relation which its subject bears to that term's primary referent. Aristotle's example is 'healthy.'[25] Thus, blood is called healthy not because it really is healthy but because it is the sign of physical well-being in an organism. Note that this derived sense of 'healthy' i.e. "being the sign of physical well-being in an organism" includes both the primary sense of 'healthy' (the idea of physical well-being) and the primary referent of 'healthy' (an organism). And as it is with 'healthy' so is it with 'true.' 'True' applies to non-judgments in a derived sense. That sense includes the primary sense and referent of 'true' just as 'healthy' in 'healthy blood' includes the primary sense and referent of 'healthy.' Thus, friends are called true not because they really are true any more than blood is called healthy because it really is healthy. Instead, they are called true because they are persons about whom a true judgment can be made, say, "These persons are friends." Here again, the derived sense of 'true,' in this case, "being persons about whom a judgment that corresponds to fact can be made" includes both the primary sense of 'true,' i.e. "corresponds to fact" and the primary referent of 'true' i.e. a judgment. Generalizing on this, one can state the principle of *pros hen* equivocity (PPE) as follows:

PPE
For any predicate P, P is attributed to a subject S equivocally *pros hen* just when the sense of P includes some relation which S bears to the primary referent of P.

NARROWNESS OF THE ARISTOTELIAN VIEW

In the view of Aquinas, this Aristotelian view of truth is one-sided.[26] It emphasizes the truth of theory to the exclusion of the truth of practice or the truth of things. The narrowness consists in defining secondary truth only, ignoring primary truth which for Aquinas is the conformity of things to their divine exemplars.[27]

True, theoretical truth is always a matter of mind's being measured by things, of mind's conformity to things. Here the bearer of 'true' and 'false' is a judgment or proposition. And though for Aquinas propositions are properly and not just elliptically called true, it is wrong, according to him, to infer from this that truth is *defined* as the correspondence of mind or judgment to thing or fact. For we saw that besides theoretical truth there is also practical truth or the truth of things, and here the conformity runs the other way. Mind measures things and not *vice versa*. In human productive truth true artifacts are ones that conform to their ideal models, and in moral truth one's statements conform to one's beliefs. But as Aquinas states, truth in the essential and primary sense is the conformity of created things to their archetypes in the divine mind.[28] That implies that even propositions have truth in this primary ontological sense of conforming to the Idea of them in God's mind, and that their truth in this sense is prior to their being true in the special sense of conforming to things or to fact.[29] Says Aquinas,

> ... A proposition not only has truth, as other things are said to have it, namely, in so far as they correspond to that which is the design of the divine intellect concerning them, but it is said to have truth in a special way, in so far as it indicates the truth of the intellect, which consists in the conformity of the intellect with a thing....[30]

Yet it is important to see that both senses of truth here are proper senses and not truth in some derived sense, even though truth as conformity of thing to divine idea is the primary sense of truth. Like every other created thing, our intellects are (ontologically) true to the extent that they conform to the Idea of the human intellect in God's mind. Moreover, since the human intellect in act is something whose form is identified with the form of another,[31] then the Idea of the human intellect in God's mind is that of something whose form is the form of another. That implies that to the extent that our intellects are ontologically true or conform to the Idea of them in God's mind as what has the form of another, they are *ipso facto* logically true or conform to things. And *vice versa*, to the extent that our intellects are logically true or conform to another, i.e. to things, they are *ipso facto* ontologically true as well. So in the view of Aquinas, it cannot be said that strictly speaking the conformity in which truth consists runs in one direction only, i.e. from mind to thing and not from thing to mind. It is arbitrary to identify proper truth with the truth of theory, thereby making the truth of practice or of things parasitic upon the truth of theory. Truth properly so called is not the conformity of mind *to* thing (or for that matter as the conformity of thing *to* mind) but the conformity of mind *and* thing.[32] Since it allows the conformity to run in either direction, this definition is wide enough to accommodate both the truth of judgment and the truth of things, i.e. mind as measured and mind as measure.

A counterexample shows not only the narrowness of Aristotle's view but also the priority of the truth of things to the truth of propositions. Suppose that DaVinci makes several *Mona Lisas* which he rejects before completing the true one. Suppose too that he points to the latter and says to friends, "That one is the true *Mona Lisa*." His statement is propositionally true. Yet it is a condition of the truth of his statement that the word 'true' which the statement contains is used *non-propositionally* to mean "conforms to my ideal model." If the painting were not true in that non-propositional sense, but was instead one of DaVinci's rejects, then DaVinci's statement would be propositionally false and not true. But under the received view it is just the other way around. All non-propositional senses of 'true' are derived from and hence conditioned by the strict propositional sense of 'true' Thus, something is called true gold only because a true judgment can be made about it, i.e. "That is gold." That is because under that view 'true' applies straightforwardly to judgments or propositions alone and to everything else only by reference to judgments or propositions. Since, therefore, *non-propositional truth is sometimes a condition of propositional truth* as our counterexample shows, then it cannot be said that the former is always derived from and conditioned by the latter. And that implies that the definition of truth as the conformity of mind to thing is too narrow. Instead, we should say with Aquinas that it is the conformity of mind and thing.

The same is shown from the standpoint of falsehood.[33] When DaVinci tells friends that one of the botched attempts they see is a false and not the true one, it is evident what he means here by 'true' and 'false.' He calls the one true because it conforms to his idea whereas he calls the one they see false because it does not. True, his botch might induce in one who views it the false judgment, "That is the *Mona Lisa*." But that is not what DaVinci means by calling it false. Besides, that judgment is one which neither DaVinci himself nor anyone else can possibly make about the botch. Since he is directly acquainted with his own ideal model, DaVinci cannot be wrong about whether or not one of his works matches it. On this point he is infallible. Nor can anyone else besides DaVinci make the false judgment in question either with or without the knowledge that what they see is a botch. Not *with* that knowledge since in that case the judgment in question contradicts what they know is the case. And not *without* that knowledge either. For unacquainted with both the real *Mona Lisa* and DaVinci's idea of it, they can no more judge that what they see is the *Mona Lisa* than I, who am ignorant both of the real *Athene* and Phidias's idea of it, can judge that what I see is Phidias's *Athene*. In either case the judgment cannot even arise. But then Aristotle's view that truth is said of non-judgments like works of art only elliptically implies this absurdity: that DaVinci's botch is called false because it is related to a judgment which no one can possibly make.

If all of this is true, then it cannot be said that, when called false, any non-judgment *whatsoever* includes in its sense some reference to a false judgment. But going by PPE, that is in fact the case if 'false' (and 'true') are *pros hen* equivocal terms that apply strictly to judgments alone. It follows that 'true' and 'false' do not apply properly to judgments and derivatively to everything else. Not all cases in which 'false' (and hence 'true') are attributed to non-judgments conform to PPE, in which case Aristotle's view is too narrow.

Yet the broader Thomistic view that truth is the conformity of mind *and* thing keeps the idea that truth is in minds and not in things. When the latter are called true, they are so called after truth which strictly speaking resides in the ideal exemplars to which they conform. To recall our example of Da Vinci who asks friends to view the true *Mona Lisa* and not his mistakes, it is clear that he calls it true after the truth of his ideal model. If in this way the truth of something is measured by another, then it is secondarily and not primarily true, according to Aquinas. For him, only what is in no respect measured by another has truth primarily speaking.[34]

That yields four *prima facie* possibilities: (i) proper, primary truth, (ii) proper, secondary truth, (iii) improper, secondary truth and (iv) improper, primary truth. Of these, only the first three are real possibilities. For what is improperly speaking true, such as my skiff or any other non-mental thing, is called true only because it is related to what is properly speaking true, say, an idea or judgment. But what is primarily speaking true is not called true only because it is related to something else that is true. It is true on its own account.

Even so, though ideal patterns like my model of the skiff are properly speaking true, they are nonetheless secondarily speaking true. For while they measure the works that mimic them, they are for their part measured. But nothing the truth of which is in any way caused or measured by another is primarily speaking true.[35] And that this is true of artists' ideas is obvious. For even though they measure and are not measured by their corresponding artifacts, these ideal models are grounded in ideas that are drawn from experience. However creative it might be, my model of the skiff is not *a priori*. It is derived from the various skiffs and their parts which I have seen. Similarly, true judgments such as my belief that silver melts at 960.5 degrees are caused or measured by corresponding facts.

Yet unlike ideal models which measure their works, true judgments in no way measure the facts they mirror. It is not our judgments that measure facts; it is facts that measure our judgments. So while they are like ideal models in being properly speaking true, true judgments fall below ideal models in their degree of truth. For their truth is made by things and not *vice versa*. Just because it is caused and not a cause or measure, therefore, theoretical truth ranks lower than practical truth in this hierarchy of truth. In fact, from the standpoint of its being a cause or measure, Aquinas, for one, ranks our judgments last among things that are called true.[36] For their truth is always effect and never cause. Ideal models cause artifacts and facts cause the truth of our judgments. But our true judgments do not cause facts. The third combination (iii) above) is improper and secondary truth. As was implied, all artifacts fall under (iii). Being things and not minds, they are called true only elliptically, i.e. only because they reflect truth. And the truth each one reflects is the mental model after which it is patterned. Moreover, just because they are effects of these same models, all artifacts are secondarily and not primarily speaking true.

TRUTH AND KNOWLEDGE

Theoretical knowledge is evidently in minds. And like theoretical truth, it is the conformity of mind to thing.[37] When for Aquinas I know either what a thing is or that something is the case, my idea or judgment matches reality. So the question is, how in Aquinas's view are theoretical and practical truth related, respectively, to theoretical and practical knowledge?

The answer is mixed. Though truth is wider than its corresponding knowledge in theoretical truth, knowledge is wider than its corresponding truth in practical truth. In theoretical truth, knowledge is equivalent to truth in simple apprehension but not in true judgment. Suppose that I have a true concept of a condor, so that my idea of it corresponds to what condors are. Then I evidently know what a condor is. Conversely, if I know what a condor is then there is conceptual truth. My concept of the bird corresponds to the bird itself. So when it concerns the truth of concepts, truth is equivalent to its corresponding knowledge i.e. knowledge of things or knowledge-*what*. But in the truth of judgment, in which theoretical truth properly consists,[38] truth and knowledge are inequivalent. Suppose that I know that Jones is at home. Then it is true that he is at home. However, suppose that I truly judge that Jones is at home. Then, unlike the truth of concepts, no corresponding knowledge is implied. For I might have mere true belief that he is at home.

Yet since for Aquinas knowledge is the effect of truth, then whenever there is truth there is also *some* sort of knowledge.[39] Thus, if my judgment that Jones is at home is true, then, even though I might not know that this is the case, I nonetheless know or am acquainted with Jones. If, trying to recall the melting point of metals, I judge truly that silver melts at 960.5 degrees, then, even though I might only believe and not know that this is the case (my memory might be faulty), I nonetheless have some knowledge of what silver is. So any true judgment on the part of a person R implies that R simply apprehends or has some conceptual knowledge of the subject of that judgment, in this case silver.

In practical truth, it is both the same and different. It is the same in that practical truth is sometimes equivalent to its corresponding knowledge and sometimes not. To recur again to DaVinci, suppose that he calls his *Mona Lisa* (practically) true because it matches his ideal model. That implies that he knows or is acquainted with both artifact and model. Yet it does not work the other way around. For since DaVinci evidently knows his ideal model even before (and as a condition of) his replicating it on canvass, then there is no conformity of artifact to model. For the artifact (in this case the *Mona Lisa*) does not yet exist.[40] But since it is just in this conformity of artifact to model that practical truth consists, it follows that there is here practical or artistic knowledge without practical or artistic truth. That shows the difference between theoretical and practical truth. In the former, though there can be truth without a corresponding knowledge, there is no knowledge of either things or facts without a corresponding truth, i.e. conceptual and judgmental, respectively. But in the latter, there can be knowledge without truth since artists know their own ideal models even before they produce them in reality.

In summary: neither theoretical nor practical truth is always equivalent to its corresponding knowledge. Yet the difference between the two types of truth is this: that whereas in theoretical truth there can be truth without the corresponding knowledge but not *vice versa*, in practical truth it is the other way around. There can be knowledge without the corresponding truth but not *vice versa*. So whereas in the domain of theory truth is wider than its corresponding knowledge, in the domain of practice knowledge is wider than its corresponding truth.

The relation between truth and knowledge in both theoretical and practical truth having been fixed, it remains to specify the interrelation, in the domain of theory, between knowing that P (and hence truly judging that P) and knowing truth or the conformity of our judgments to things.[41] Toward that end, let it be assumed that it is better for mind to know that-P than merely to believe that-P. Thus, from seeing it work out in a few cases, I might truly believe (but not yet know) that the sum of two consecutive numbers (1,2,3, etc.) equals the difference between the squares of those numbers (1,4,9, etc.). When I go from believing to knowing this by grasping the formula behind the individual cases, i.e. $2n + 1 = (n + 1)^2 - n^2$, then my mind improves on its prior state of mere belief. Mind is improved by knowing as over against merely truly believing. But in addition, mind improves even further when, due to this newly acquired knowledge, mind knows not just the rule but its own truth or conformity to the rule.[42] Mind thus indirectly or reflexively knows its own conformity to reality by knowing reality. That explains Aquinas's identifying the end or perfection of mind not with either truth or knowledge as such but with the richer synthesis of both. This is truth *as known*.[43] The end of mind is not true judgments but judgments known to be true. And this occurs, says he, when intellect knows "its own conformity to the thing known." (Intellectus autem conformitatem sui ad rem intelligibilem cognoscere potest; ...)[44] Says Aquinas,

> ...There is truth and falsity, then, only in the second operation of the intellect, according to which it not only possesses a likeness of the thing known *but also reflects on this likeness by knowing it (i.e. the likeness) and by making a judgment about it*....[45]

This truth as known evidently implies and is implied by both truth and knowledge-*that*. When I truly believe but do not know the foregoing mathematical rule, then I have no acquaintance with the conformity of my judgment of the rule to the fact that makes it true. In other words, I lack *known* truth. Otherwise I should know and not just truly believe the rule. When, however, I go from truly believing to knowing that rule, then and only then do I see the conformity of my judgment to the mathematical fact that makes it true. For if I am unacquainted with the conformity of my judgment to the fact, I should not know but only truly believe the rule.

Thus does mind advance in three stages in its relation to the rule in question. First, it goes from ignorance of the rule to true belief of it. Second, it moves from mere true belief of the rule to knowing the rule. Finally, in and through its knowing the rule, mind knows its own truth or the conformity of its judgment to the rule. So mind advances from having true judgment about the rule to both having that judgment and knowing its conformity to the rule. This meta-knowledge or truth as known fulfills the third stage which is mind's knowledge of its own conformity to reality. In between is the second stage in which mind moves from truly believing the rule to knowing it, and this advancement is both necessary and sufficient for the final stage of its knowing its own truth or conformity to the rule. Since in this final stage mind simultaneously possesses not just truth but both first-order knowledge of fact and second-order knowledge of truth, mind is perfected as over against its first two stages. ("...perfectio enim intellectus est verum ut cognitum.")[46]

Another example of the equivalence of truth as known and knowledge-*that* is this: when I am acquainted with the conformity of my judgment, "A whole is greater than one of its parts" to the fact in question, there is both truth (i.e. the truth of that judgment) and my knowledge that a whole is greater than one of its parts. Since no one knows the conformity between two things without knowing those things, then no one knows the conformity of one's judgment to fact without knowing that fact. Conversely, suppose that I know — and do not just truly believe — that the whole is greater than one of its parts. Then this knowledge of fact evidently implies that I know the conformity of my judgment, "A whole is greater than one of its parts" to fact or that I possess known truth. Otherwise I should merely believe and not know that dictum. And so it is that while the truth of any judgment or proposition P implies neither one's knowledge that-P nor one's acquaintance with the truth of P, one's knowledge that-P for its part both implies and is implied by the conjunct of P's truth together with one's acquaintance with that truth. In summary, if 1) truth as known occurs only if there is knowledge-*that* as opposed to mere true belief, and 2) if knowledge-*that*, as opposed to mere true belief, for its part implies truth as known and hence truth, then it follows that truth as known is equivalent to knowledge-*that*.

PRIMARY TRUTH AS IDENTIFIED WITH GOD

In the hierarchy of truth that was listed in section II ((i)-(iv) above), the highest truth is (i). This truth that is in mind and yet uncaused is identified with divine truth. It is the conformity of natural things to their archetypes in God's mind. Though natural things measure our minds, they are in turn measured by divine Ideas.[47] As artists' models measure artifacts, so do divine Ideas measure natural things. The difference is that while artists' models are in some way measured, divine Ideas are totally unmeasured. Otherwise something causes or measures God. Though all non-theists as well as theists of a nominalist stripe shun divine Ideas, proof of them is possible.[48] Combining elements from Plato and Aristotle, one such proof is implicit in the metaphysics of Aquinas. In the spirit of Plato, it proceeds from things that are participatively F to something that is non-participatively F. But departing from Plato, it shows that the latter is no separated Form but a mind-dependent Idea where the mind in question is God's.

To spell it out, to say that two things share or participate in some form F means for Aquinas that neither one of them is identical with F. Instead, each one is a composite of F and what participates in F. The latter is matter or potentiality. For what participates is related to that in which it participates as matter or potentiality is related to form or act.[49] By contrast, something is or has form non-participatively just when it is identified with its form. Recall Plato's Forms. They are each one of them form alone and do not have this other thing, matter, joined to them as the potential to the actual.

If *a* is participatively F, then the form F, though possibly essential to *a*, is accidental to the matter in *a* that participates in it.[50] Take Freda the fox. Though the form of fox is essential to Freda, it is accidental to the matter in Freda which participates in that form. Otherwise matter is essentially form and in particular the form of foxhood. However, if form of any kind is accidental to matter, then it is caused to be in matter by something else. The latter is some efficient cause which makes matter acquire the form in question. By analogy, since being 100 degrees Fahrenheit is accidental to water, then water's being that temperature is due to some external efficient cause, say, fire.

This cause of *a*'s primal matter taking on some form F is not some other individual F-thing (say *b*) which, like *a*, participates in F. In our example, what causes the matter in Freda to take on or assume the form of fox is not another fox, say, Frances. For like Freda's matter, Frances' matter also takes on or assumes the form of fox, and the latter is accidental to Frances' matter just as it is to Freda's. Otherwise matter is essentially form and in particular the form of fox. And our question is, what causes the matter in any arbitrarily selected individual *y* to take on or assume some form which is accidental to it? To this the answer evidently is not some other individual that is participatively F. For no less than that of the first, the matter of this second individual takes on F-ness which is accidental to it. It is added onto it, as it were, from the outside. But since it is just this addition *per accidens* that must be explained, any such "explanation" of one such addition by another begs the question. A is not explained by B when B is either the same as or includes A. No *explanatio* is or includes the *explanatum* without circularity. If, then, the cause of matter's taking on F in *a* cannot be said to be another thing *b* that is also participatively F, then with what is that cause identified?

The answer is evidently what is *both* an efficient cause and non-participatively F. Something is required to make matter take on form and that can only be an efficient cause. By analogy, something is required to make a block of marble into the *Athene* and that can only be an efficient cause, in this case Phidias, or more exactly, Phidias as sculpturing. That excludes a Platonic Form as the cause of matter's being F in *a*. For to identify the required non-participative F here with a Platonic Form falsely substitutes a formal for an efficient cause. Recall that Plato installed the Demiurge to explain matter's being F in *a*. He saw that what is required for this is an efficient cause.[51] Yet what the Demiurge has on the one side it lacks on the other. For besides being efficient cause, the cause of matter's being F in *a* must be non-participatively F, and the Demiurge is not. Plato's Forms are separated not just from their copies but also from the Demiurge who makes those copies. What meets both criteria is something that is at once agent-cause and non-participatively F. As both agent-cause and non-participatively F, such a being is the Thomistic God.

SUMMARY

It was shown that for Aquinas, the Aristotelian idea of truth as the conformity of mind to thing is too narrow. More broadly, truth for him is the conformity of mind and thing[52], a definition which allows the conformity to run in both directions, i.e. from mind to thing in theoretical truth and from thing to mind in practical truth. Moreover, in adopting this broader definition of truth Aquinas would seem to be justified. For as our example of DaVinci shows, the truth of things is sometimes a condition of the truth of judgment. But no account of this is possible under the view that the truth of things is derivative of the truth of judgment. Second, it was shown that since for Aquinas truth of any sort requires two terms, mind and thing, then in practical or productive truth there can be knowledge without truth. For artists know their own ideal models even when nothing as yet exemplifies those models. For they know those models even before they make the artifacts that are modeled after them. Therefore, whereas practical or productive truth implies knowledge of ideal models, the latter does not imply practical or productive truth. However, in theoretical truth it is the other way around. Since it might express mere true belief as well as knowledge, judgmental truth does not imply knowledge-*that*. However, knowledge-*that does* imply judgmental truth. Third, I showed that while for Aquinas the truth of any judgment or proposition P implies neither one's knowledge that-P nor one's acquaintance with the truth of P, yet, one's knowledge that-P both implies and is implied by the conjunct of P's truth together with one's acquaintance with that truth. Finally, it was shown that Aquinas is right in holding that truth in the primary sense of unmeasured measure is identified with God. For things that are participatively F can only be caused by what is non-participatively F, and this cause must be an efficient as well as an exemplary cause. This unmeasured measure is therefore no separated Form but can only be the Thomistic God who, viewed as participable by creatures, is identified with His divine Ideas.

NOTES

1. St. Thomas Aquinas, *De veritate*, I, 1, in James F. Anderson, trans. *An Introduction to the Metaphysics of St. Thomas Aquinas* (Chicago: Henry Regnery Co., 1953), 46.
2. Ibid., *De veritate*, I, 1., in James F. Anderson, trans., 45
3. Ibid., *De veritate*, XXI, 1., in James F. Anderson, trans., 77.
4. Ibid., *De veritate* XXI, 1, in James F. Anderson, trans., 76.
5. Aristotle, *Metaphysics*, trans. W.D. Ross, in R. McKeon, ed., *The Basic Works of Aristotle* (New York: Random House, 1941) 1021a 30–5, 769.
6. St. Thomas Aquinas, *De veritate*, q. I, a. 2, in James F. Anderson, trans., 67.
7. St. Thomas Aquinas, *Commentary on the Metaphysics of Aristotle* trans. J. P. Rowan (Chicago: Henry Regnery Co.1961), vol. I, III. L.4: C #375, 154.
8. St. Thomas Aquinas, *Summa theologica* in *Introduction to St. Thomas Aquinas*, trans. A. Pegis (New York: The Modern Library, 1948) I, q.16, a. 2, 171-172.
9. St. Thomas Aquinas, *De veritate*, XXI, 1., in James F. Anderson, trans., 77.
10. St. Thomas Aquinas, *Commentary on the Metaphysics of Aristotle*, vol. II, VI. L.4:C 1239, 482–83.
11. St. Thomas Aquinas, *Summa theologica*, trans. A. Pegis I q. 16, a. 4, 174–175.
12. Ibid., *Summa theologica,* trans. A. Pegis I q. 16, a. 4, reply obj. 1., 175.
13. Aquinas states that if our intellects did not exist, things would still be said to be true in relation to God's intellect. In the same context, he says that truth is primarily and properly in God's intellect and secondarily (though properly) in our intellects, and that truth is by priority said of things in relation to God's intellect and not ours. Since God's intellect is not true because it conforms to things, this shows that Aquinas would view the definition of truth as the conformity of intellect to thing as too narrow since it applies only to judgmental truth in us and

not to truth in God. See St. Thomas Aquinas, *De veritate*, trans. by R. Mulligan, S.J. (Chicago: Henry Regnery, 1952), vol. I, q. I, a. 2, 10–12.

14. By 'degrees of truth' here it is not meant that judgments are to a degree true and to a degree false depending on how adequately they express the Absolute or the whole-of-reality. Aquinas would reject this Hegelian notion of degrees of truth. What he means is (i) that to the extent that they are measured by things, our ideas (judgments included) have truth to a lesser degree than do divine Ideas which are not in any way measured but which are the measure of things and (ii) that among our true judgments, those in which the truth is known by us have a higher degree of truth than those in which it is unknown.

15. St. Thomas Aquinas, *De veritate*, trans. R. Mulligan, S.J. (Chicago: Henry Regnery, 1952), vol. I, q.1, a.1, 5.

16. Ibid., *De veritate*, trans. R. Mulligan, S.J., q.1, a.1, reply to obj. 6 and 7, 8.

17. Ibid., *De veritate*, trans. R. Mulligan, S.J., q.1, a.1, 6.

18. In what follows I show that this conformity in which truth consists runs in both directions, i.e. from thing to intellect and from intellect to thing.

19. St. Thomas Aquinas, *Summa theologiae*, trans. Thomas Gilby, O.P. (London: Blackfriars, in conjunction with Eyre & Spottiswoode, 1964) Ia, q.16 a.1, vol. IV, 74–79. In the case of theoretical truth, the source to which mind corresponds is the real or non-mental. In the case of practical truth, whether it concerns natural things or artifacts, the source to which these things correspond (and in which truth properly speaking resides) is mind, whether divine or human.

20. The causality here is indirect. The real condor is impressed on the sense power to form a phantasm which in turn causes the concept of a condor only through the abstractive power of the agent intellect. See St. Thomas Aquinas, *Summa theologiae*, trans. Thomas Gilby, O.P., Ia q. 85, a. 1, reply to 3, vol. XII, 53–56.

21. Practical truth or the truth of making includes the truth of things or what in the tradition is called ontological truth as well as the truth of artifacts in human making. Like artifacts, natural things are also called true in a secondary and extended sense, i.e. because they conform to their respective ideal models. But the latter are identified with divine and not human models or ideas.

22. St. Thomas Aquinas, *De veritate*, trans. R. Mulligan, S.J., q. I, a. 2, 11.

23. As opposed to the later medieval thinker, William of Ockham, all these medieval realists recognized ontological as well as propositional truth, the former being the conformity of natural things to their divine Exemplars.

24. Aristotle, *Categoriae*, trans. E.M. Edghill, in R. McKeon, ed., *The Basic Works of Aristotle* (New York: Random House, 1941), Chapter 12, 14b, 14–22, 35.; St. Thomas Aquinas, *Summa contra gentiles*, trans. A. Pegis (Garden City, N.Y: Doubleday & Co., Inc., 1955), Book I Chapter 59, no. 2, 201.

25. Aristotle, *Metaphysics*, trans. W. D. Ross, in R. McKeon, ed., *The Basic Works of Aristotle* (New York: Random House, 1941) Book IV, 2, 1003a32–b5, 732; Book XI, 3,1060b36–1061a7, 854.

26. This is shown by Aquinas's belief that truth is primarily speaking found only in God in Whom there is no knowledge by judgments. This divine truth consists in God's being the Exemplar and measure of creatures. Therefore Aquinas regards our judgmental truth as secondary truth. See St. Thomas Aquinas, *De veritate*, trans. R. Mulligan, S.J., q. 1, a. 2, 11.

27. Ibid., *De veritate*, trans. R. Mulligan, S.J., q. 1, a.2, 11.

28. Ibid., *De veritate*, trans. R. Mulligan, S.J. q. 1, a. 2, p. 11. See also, Aquinas, *Summa theologiae* trans. Thomas Gilby, O.P. Ia q. 16, a. 1, vol. IV, 76–77.

29. Ibid., *Summa theologiae*, trans. Thomas Gilby, O.P., Ia, q. 16, a. 8, reply to obj. 3, 98–99.

30. Ibid., *Summa theologiae*, trans. Thomas Gilby, O.P., Ia, q. 16, a. 8, reply to obj. 3, 98–99.

31. Ibid., *Summa theologiae*, trans. Thomas Gilby, O.P., I, q. 16, a. 2, 81.

32. Aquinas defines truth as the equation or adequation of thought and thing, which is wide enough to include both the truth of propositions and the truth of things. See Aquinas, *Summa theologiae*, trans. Thomas Gilby, O.P. Ia q. 16, a. 1, vol. IV, 78–79.

68 Chapter 4

33. From this standpoint, I have previously argued for the same conclusion. See my "Conceptualism and Truth," *Ratio*, vol. XII, No. 3, September, 2000, 237–38.

34. St. Thomas Aquinas, *De veritate*, trans. R. Mulligan, S.J., q. 1, a. 2, 11.

35. Aquinas holds that truth is primarily and properly speaking found in God alone. See St. Thomas Aquinas, *De veritate*, trans. R. Mulligan, S.J., q. 1 a. 4, 17.

36. St. Thomas Aquinas, *De veritate*, trans. R. Mulligan, S.J., q. I, a. 2, 11.

37. As to theoretical truth and knowledge, Aquinas holds that knowledge of a thing follows truth or the assimilation of the intellect to the thing known, so that knowledge is the effect of truth. (see Aquinas, *De veritate*, trans. R. Mulligan, S.J. q. I, a.1). Therefore, where there is any kind of theoretical truth (i.e. either judgmental or conceptual truth) there is some kind of theoretical knowledge (i.e. either knowledge-that or knowledge-what), and where there is any kind of theoretical knowledge (i.e. either knowledge-that or knowledge-what) there is some kind of theoretical truth (i.e. either judgmental or conceptual truth).

38. St. Thomas Aquinas, *De veritate*, trans. R. Mulligan, q. 1, a. 3, 13; *Summa theologiae*, trans. Thomas Gilby, O.P. Ia q. 16, a. 2, vol. IV, 78–81.

39. Ibid., *De veritate*, trans. R. Mulligan, q. 1 a. 1.

40. Aquinas states that an artist sometimes produces a form which is modeled after an exemplar which is interiorly conceived in his mind as opposed to modeling it after an external exemplar. See Aquinas, *Summa theologica*, trans. A. Pegis I, q. 44, a. 3, 238–239.

41. Aquinas states that intellect knows its own truth in reflecting on its own act, not just as knowing its own act but also as knowing the proportion of its act to the thing. See St. Thomas Aquinas, *De veritate*, trans. R. Mulligan, q. I a. 9, 41.

42. This is consistent with Maritain's view that mind knows its own truth when it resolves thought "into the immediate assertions of sensible experience and *the first principles of the understanding in which our knowledge cannot be false*...." (italics mine). I extend this to include necessary truths besides the first principles of understanding. See Jacques Maritain, *The Degrees of Knowledge* trans, G. Phelan (New York: Charles Scribner's Sons, 1959), 89. For an interpretation of Maritain's analysis of knowing truth in Aquinas, see J.C. Cahalan, "The Problem of Thing and Object in Maritain," *The Thomist*, vol. 59, 1, January, 1995, 36–39.

43. St. Thomas Aquinas, *Summa theologiae*, trans. Thomas Gilby, O.P., Ia q. 16 a. 2, vol. IV, 80–81.

44. Ibid.

45. St. Thomas Aquinas, *Commentary on the Metaphysics of Aristotle*, trans. J.P. Rowan (Chicago:1961, Henry Regnery Co.), vol II, no. 1236, 482. (emphasis and parentheses mine).

46. St. Thomas Aquinas, *Summa theologiae*, trans. Thomas Gilby, O.P., Ia q. 16 a. 2, vol. IV, 80–81.

47. St. Thomas Aquinas, *De veritate*, trans. R. Mulligan, S.J., q 1, a. 2, 11.

48. For further discussion of this proof see my *Aquinas: A New Introduction* (Lanham, Md: University Press of America, 2008), 63–73; 80–82.

49. St. Thomas Aquinas, *Summa contra gentiles*, trans. J.F. Anderson (New York: Doubleday & Co., Inc., 1956), Book Two: Creation, Chapter 53, no. 4, 156.

50. For purposes of the argument, I assume hylomorphism, i.e. that the changing things of our experience are composed of primal matter and substantial form. Defense of this Aristotelian view is beyond the scope of this chapter.

51. Plato, *Timaeus*, in *The Dialogues of Plato*, trans. B. Jowett (Oxford: The Clarendon Press, 1953), vol. III, (28a–29a), 716.

52. St. Thomas Aquinas, *De veritate*, trans. R. Mulligan, q. 1 a. 4, reply to 1; *Summa theologiae*, trans. Thomas Gilby, O.P., Ia q. 16 a. 1, 74–79.

Chapter Five

Persons

I

In ordinary language we speak of *our* bodies as if we are not identical with them but possess them or have them as aspects of ourselves. Is this only a way of speaking? Or language apart, are we really identified with our bodies? Does language here signify a real difference between ourselves and our bodies? And if it does, how is that difference to be construed or how are we related to our bodies?

These questions express the mind-body issue in philosophy, and for our present purposes the question is how Aquinas stands on this issue. Since both questions presuppose the idea of a person, one must ask how Aquinas construes a person. Only then can one assess how he would regard or answer the mind-body problem. Moreover, this is only as it should be since for Aquinas the idea of a mind or a (human) body is a kind of abstraction from the more concrete notion of a person. Thinking is not a function of a thing called a mind or a thing called a body for Aquinas, nor is walking, say, an activity of either one of these things. The former is a function of a person and the latter is an activity of a person.

Aquinas's view of persons opposes four alternative accounts. These are identity materialism, standard dualism (whether interactionist or not) epiphenomenalism and idealism. Under the first, persons are identified with their bodies. According to the second, persons are composed of two irreducible things or substances, i.e. a body and an immaterial mind. Under the third, though persons are fundamentally their bodies, what we call a person's mental events are different in kind from his or her bodily events. Yet all mental or psychological events in a person supervene upon his or her bodily events and cannot occur without the latter. According to the fourth, persons are identified with their immaterial minds, their bodies being either non-existent or else accidental to and directed by their minds.

In common with standard dualists and against identity materialists, Aquinas denies that persons are identified with their bodies. Yet with identity materialists and as against standard dualists, St. Thomas denies that persons are composed of two things, a thing we call the body and another thing we call the mind. He opposed Plato's idea of a person,[1] i.e. that persons are their immaterial souls which move and direct their bodies as things which are accidental to them, and he also would have opposed Descartes dualism as well. At the same time, with dualists and against epiphenomenalists, Aquinas denies that intellectual operations like conceiving, judging and reasoning are intrinsically dependent on the body. Further, with dualists and against epiphenomenalists (to the extent that the latter admit any such thing as a mind), he denies that what he calls the mind or intellect of a person is the effect of that person's body. To the contrary, he holds that the human body is what it is because of the human intellectual soul. For he follows Aristotle in holding that the soul is the substantial form of the body. Since for him it is the form of an individual material thing that makes it exist and not its matter, then it is the soul that makes an individual human body exist. It is also a thing's substantial form and not its matter that makes it what it is.

Yet there are differences between the Aristotelian and Thomistic accounts of the person. However, putting these aside for the moment, let us see how Aquinas gets between all four of these positions (i.e. identity materialism, standard dualism, epiphenomenalism, idealism) to forge a fifth view.

To show this, I begin with judgment. I argue that the logic of judgment and in particular the predicable relations of genus, difference and species exclude all four answers. What is not excluded but is implied by those relations is a fifth response. It is that an individual human body is a complex of form and matter in which the former is identified with that body's soul. Thus is this soul a constituent and co-cause of the body. It is not itself a body but the substantial form of a human body. Moreover, it is the source of all those functions and relations, including the predicable relations of genus, species, etc. which we characterize as being mental as opposed to physical. Just for that reason can this soul be called mind, though it is far from being mind in either a Platonic or Cartesian sense. This hylomorphic or Aristotelian view of a person is evidently neither identity materialism, standard dualism, epiphenomenalism nor idealism. It is reflected in the logic of ordinary judgments. To bring all this out, I begin with the predicable relations in logic.

Among the five predicables Aquinas distinguishes genus, difference and species. These are evidently relations like employer, sibling, client, etc. As an employer is necessarily the employer of an employee and a sibling by definition the sibling of a sister or brother, so too is a genus necessarily the genus *of* species and a species necessarily the species *of* individuals. Moreover, it is also evident that genus and species are logical and not real relations. For one thing, predicables like genus and species are subjects or predicates of judgments. Thus, in the judgment, "The whale is a mammal," the subject is the species whale and the predicate is the genus mammal. But subjects and predicates, like the judgments which include them, are logical and not real entities. Besides, genera and species are devices we use in judgment to refer some part of a thing to the whole of which it is the part. Thus, by means of the genus mammal in the foregoing judgment, I refer part of what a whale is, i.e. a mammal, to the whole that is signified by the species. However, though the facts to which true judgments correspond are real, the judgments by which we signify them are not. In no real whole does a part of it stand apart from it. Nor is that part at the same time referred back to the whole. Yet in judgments, predicates both stand apart from their subjects and refer back to those subjects.[2] This simultaneous analysis and synthesis is all the work of reason. But if judgments are thus beings of reason, then so too are the subjects and predicates that comprise them, including judgments by genus and species. Thus, in judging that whales are mammals, we use the genus-concept *mammal* as a mental device to predicate the real character of being a mammal of the thing signified by the species-concept, *whale*. Similarly, in judging that Willy is a whale, we use the species-concept *whale* as a logical tool to predicate the real nature of being a whale of the individual named by the subject, "Willy."

Though they are similar in some ways, predicables are not classes or sets. Like classes, genera and species are non-physical. No more than a genus or species is a class a group of physical things, like a group of pigeons on the grass. Nor is a class a transcendent or subsistent entity like a Platonic Form either. For suppose that the class of humans is such a timeless thing. Then so too are its members. For the members of a class are not outside that class but belong to it. And it is difficult to see how either real individuals or ideas of them can possibly belong to or be members of a timeless entity. The only way to avoid this is to posit timeless individual humans as members of the timeless class of humans. But then we all of us have a twin in a Platonic heaven. And this, though not impossible, is unbelievable. So it seems that, like genera and species, classes or sets are mental or logical constructions.

Yet to think that they are just different names for the same thing is mistaken. The easiest way to show this is from null-classes. There are null-classes like the class of mermaids and the class of Martians. But the idea of a null-species is a contradiction in terms. For we saw that, being by definition relational, a species is necessarily the species *of* individuals just as a genus is necessarily the genus *of* species. This shows the basic difference between a class and a species. And that is that species are by definition intentional while classes are not. Any species is the species *of* individuals, but no class is the class *of* individuals in this intentional sense of 'of.' True, lowest level classes are necessarily classes *of* individuals as opposed to higher-level classes which are classes of classes. Unless one confuses class-membership with class-inclusion, they can be nothing else. But this is a very different sense of 'of' than the sense of 'of' in which species are said to be species of individuals or genera are said to be genera of species. What it is meant by saying that a class is a class of individuals is that the individuals belong to the class, as all of us belong to the class of humans. But what it is meant by saying that a species is necessarily a species of individuals is the converse of this, i.e. that what the species signifies belongs to the individuals, as being human belongs to or is predicated of those individuals.

This intentionality of genera and species not only marks them off from classes but it also shows how they are predicables. As genus or species in the mind, some property or nature stands apart or is abstracted from its existence in individuals. When I judge that Willy is a whale, I abstract the property or nature of being a whale both from Willy and from every other whale. For if the individuality of, say, Willy, is included in the sense of the predicate *whale*, then I evidently cannot predicate whale of Wally or of any other whale. I can predicate the property of being a whale of any and every individual whale just because none of these individuals are included in that predicate or species.

Yet the irony is this. That to predicate being a whale of Willy, Wally or any other whale, it is equally required that I not abstract whale from those individuals to the point of cutting it off from them entirely. The necessary abstraction must not go so far as to be a precision.[3] This happens when, say, I consider whaleness as a real part of, say, Willy, i.e. as something in Willy that is set off from Willy's individuality or that other part of Willy which makes him Willy. Considered as a part in this way, whale is evidently impredicable of any individual whale. No one says that any real whole (in this case Willy) is one of its parts.

To predicate whale of Willy, then, I must get between either including Willy in the sense of the predicate or entirely excluding Willy from the predicate. For the first implies that whale, if predicable at all, is predicable of Willy only; and the second implies that whale is impredicable of any individual whale, since no whole can be said to be one of its parts.

Getting between the horns of this dilemma is just what a species or any other predicable does. They do this by having both intension (sense) and extension. This duality allows the consistent synthesis that *whale* both includes and excludes Willy. It includes Willy in its extension but excludes Willy from its intension. I predicate whale of Willy, Wally, etc. because the species *whale* by which I do this lacks the individuality of any one whale in its sense. This is what is meant by abstraction. Yet I do this without judging or saying that a whole is one of its parts because this abstraction is not a precision. That means that, as a species, *whale* in the judgment, "Willy is a whale" signifies the whole and not just a part of the subject Willy. And that is because, though it excludes the individuality of Willy or any other whale from its sense or intention, the species *whale* nonetheless includes those individuals in its extension. Thus do I predicate a whole of a whole and not a part of a whole when I judge that Willy is a whale.[4]

This feature of implicit inclusion in logic parallels the feature of potentiality in reality. Individuals with some properties are never absolutely cut off from other properties but implicitly or potentially contain them. A green leaf in summer is implicitly or potentially brown. Though not actually or explicitly brown, it is not absolutely cut off from brown. Open to brown, the leaf can be said to be an open thing. Similarly, though the species *whale* no more explicitly includes Willy than the green leaf actually includes brown, it is no more absolutely cut off from Willy than the green leaf is absolutely cut off from brown. Instead, it implicitly includes Willy as the green leaf potentially includes brown. Thus is it an open concept, as the leaf is an open thing. By contrast, real greenness is never open to being brownness and so can be called a closed thing. Recall Plato's comment in the *Phaedo* that of two opposed forms "…one of them can never become the other"[5] Correspondingly, since, as a part of Willy, whaleness is impredicable of him, then the concept *whaleness* is a closed and not (like the species *whale*) an open concept. The difference is that whereas in reality it is properties which are latent in individuals, in logic it is individuals that are latent in known properties (species). Those stark dualisms that diminish some philosophies find no place either in logic or reality.

Nevertheless, though properties are latent in real individuals and individuals are latent in species in the senses specified, the terms of this latent-relation are evidently distinct in each case. After all, *one* thing is said to be latent in *another*. Individuals are not their properties nor are species the individuals they intend. If it is wrong to infer separateness from distinctness (an error, as was just implied, that is behind most hard and fast dualisms in philosophy), then it is equally wrong to infer sameness from non-separateness. You cannot infer that A and B are the same just because they are not separate. Otherwise size and shape are the same because they are inseparable.

This is illustrated in the case of body and mind. Suppose that some philosophers hold that body and mind are distinct. From this they would wrongly infer that they are separate things. Similarly, suppose that they deny that body and mind are separate things. From this they would wrongly infer that they are the same. Just because body and mind are not separate substances, it hardly follows that they are names for the same thing. Between dualism and identity materialism lie other options.

Of these, the true one is implied by the logical relations of genus and species which have just been reviewed. To see this, recall that a predicable is a relation of both conceptual analysis and synthesis in which some feature of a thing is paradoxically both abstracted from it and united to it. In judging that Willy is a whale, I pull out the property of being a whale from Willy by an act of abstractive analysis and simultaneously reunite it to Willy by an act of logical synthesis. A sign of the first is the distinction of subject and predicate, while the sign of the second is the copula 'is' by which I reunite or synthesize what I abstracted or analyzed by that distinction. So the relation of species is a logical device of both analysis and synthesis. And as it is with species, so is it with genus and difference.

These logical relations are nowhere found in my body. You will never find in the brain some property or universal which both stands apart from an individual or individuals and yet refers back to that same individual or individuals. True, some brain-event or state might correspond to these relations. But it can never *be* those relations. For no brain-event or state is or includes that relation of analysis and synthesis to which we referred. Nothing in the brain is some abstracted property which nonetheless bears the property of being linked to the individual or individuals from which it is set apart. No part of the brain or of a brain-event is or exemplifies the property of being an abstracted universal with respect to many particulars. That being the case, the existence of these logical relations of genus, difference and species imply that I, who make those relations, am identified neither with my body nor with one of its parts or activities. Under identity materialism, no account of these predicable relations is possible.

Moreover, these same predicables of logic also defeat the very opposite view, i.e. that persons are identified with their immaterial minds (idealism). To see how the predicables exclude idealism too, recall that a species includes a genus in its sense but not *vice versa*. Hence, the species includes something that is not included in the genus. This is the difference which is outside of the genus. Thus, the species larch includes the genus tree but not *vice versa*. Otherwise all trees are larches. So in addition to the genus tree, the species larch includes some difference which is outside of the genus. Similarly, the species human includes both a genus and a difference.

Now among genera, some are evidently wider than others, as, for example, the genus plant is wider than the genus tree. That implies that there is a widest genus. Otherwise no genus has determinate sense. If the genus plant is wider than the genus tree and the genus organism is wider than the genus plant, and another genus is still wider than the genus organism, and so on, *ad infinitum* — so that there is no widest genus — then, since any one genus (say, tree) includes an infinite number of wider genera, then no one genus has fixed sense.[6] But since our concepts do have determinate sense, then there is a widest genus which is included in every individual thing in the world. Further, this widest or simple genus evidently does not have the nature or character of being immaterial. Otherwise, since every species includes both its proximate and remote genera (as tree includes plant, organism, etc., all the way to the widest genus), then there are no such things as bodies. But since that is unbelievable, then it follows that to the extent that they include a genus, all species (and hence the species human) include a material element. But since species are predicated of individuals, then persons are no more their minds than they are their bodies. The logic of genus, difference and species, then, defeats idealism no less than identity materialism.

Yet to continue, it seems that the predicable relations eliminate standard dualism as well as both identity materialism and idealism. This might appear surprising if not contradictory. For it was just argued that that those relations imply that persons have both a material and an immaterial side, and that is just what standard dualists claim. So the question is this. If under standard dualism persons have these two sides and if that is just what was shown to be implied by the predicable relations, then how is standard dualism *falsified* by those relations?

The key to the answer is grasping the relation between genus and difference within any composite concept. That relation is one of the conceptually unsaturated to what saturates it, i.e. of the logically unspecified to what specifies it. Thus, in the composite idea *organism*, the genus is the open or unsaturated concept *body* which is closed, limited, or saturated by the difference-concept *living*. As Aquinas notes, the genus *body* signifies something which has a form through which three dimensions characterize it, leaving it open exactly what that form is.[7] For that reason, the difference *living* is implicitly contained in the genus *body*. In other words, the relation between genus and difference is that of the logically open and implicit to what closes that openness and makes that implicitness explicit.

Now this logical relation of the open and implicit to what closes, limits and makes it explicit mirrors and is based on the real relation of the potential to what actuates it in any nature or essence that is a composite of the potential and the actual. In our example, the logical relation between the genus *body* and the difference *living* answers to the real potential–actual or matter-form relation in the thing signified by the idea *organism*. In reality something can have a form through which three dimensions can characterize it *no matter what that form is*, either merely corporeal or living. Reflecting this real openness, is a corresponding logical openness. For the genus body is susceptible of various *differentiae* through which the idea of having three dimensions can be realized. In a word, genus is to difference in our ideas what matter (potentiality) is to form (actuality) in things. Genus, difference and species in our concepts, says Aquinas, answer to matter, form and composite, respectively, in the world.[8]

It is now evident how the predicable relations of logic falsify standard dualism no less than identity materialism and idealism. For assume that logic mirrors the world such that our concepts of things always contain a genus and a difference which reflect the real relation in those things of the potential to the actual or of matter to form. Then it is wrong to say with standard dualists that a person is composed of two distinct things or substances, i.e. a mind-substance and a body-substance. Instead, like everything else in the world, a person is one thing or substance with the distinct aspects of the potential and the actual or of matter and form. What standard dualists call "the mind" or "the soul" is no substance in its own right but the formal or actual side of a substance, say, the person Socrates. And what they call "the body" is not another substance, standing, as it were, starkly opposed to the mind-substance. Instead, it is the result of the union of the formal and the material sides of a substance, say, once again, the person Socrates. For this is just what the predicable concept *human* signifies. The latter, like all our ideas of things in the world, is composed of genus and difference. But so far from its being isolated or starkly opposed to the difference, the genus implicitly contains the difference as that through which it can be realized. And together they comprise the species. Assuming, then, that logic in this way maps the world, then what the logical two-in-one or species *human* signifies is a real two-in-one, i.e. a single person in whom matter and form or the potential and the actual fit together like hand in glove.

Finally, the predicable relations are incompatible with epiphenomenlism no less than with identity materialism, idealism and standard dualism. Unlike Platonists and idealists and like Aristotelians and identity materialists, epiphenomenalists hold that being a body enters into the definition of a person. A person is no disembodied mind or soul but is a certain kind of living body. It is that kind of organism we call an animal, so that for epiphenomenalists the proximate genus of a person is *animal*. Yet epiphenomenalists recognize that persons differ from other animals by exemplifying abstract reasoning which in their view is distinct from and irreducible to matter. And in this they depart from identity materialists. They do not deny that non-human animals can think but they do deny that, due to their smaller or less intricate brains, non-human animals think on a level that matches of human thinking.

Moreover, in common with standard dualists, epiphenomenalists hold that the mental is irreducible to the physical. Yet departing from them, they insist that mental events entirely supervene on the body or bodily events. Mental events or activities could not exist unless there were certain bodily states or events which cause them. However, though some mental events might cause others, no mental event can ever cause a bodily event. The causal direction works only from the physical to the mental or from the mental to the mental but never from the mental to the physical. So epiphenomenalists hold that, though mental, the predicable relations of which we speak, i.e. genus, difference and species are all of them caused by certain physical states or events in the brain and/or nervous system.

However, it is difficult to see how this could ever be the case. For recall that in any one of the predicable relations, the predicate both pulls some feature out of the subject and refers it back to that subject. This analysis and synthesis is shown by the distinction of subject and predicate in a judgment and by their unification by the copula, respectively. Thus, in judging (by species) that Willy is a whale, I both abstract the property of being a whale from Willy and refer it back to Willy *via* the copula 'is.' And as a result of this two-fold mental relation, subject and predicate are said to be both different and the same, i.e. different in sense but the same in reference.

However, how can epiphenomenalists any more than identity materialists account for this judgment by species or for that matter a judgment by any one of the other predicables? To be reunited to the subject by an act of mental synthesis that is signified by the copula, the property signified by the predicate must have been abstracted from it by a prior act of mental analysis. That means that in judging that Willy is a whale, I possess the abstract concept of being a whale. But if the trouble identity materialists have with this is showing how some abstract concept can possibly be located in a body, the trouble that epiphenomenalists have with it is showing how either the body, which is particular and concrete, or any state or event in the body, which is also particular and concrete, can ever possibly produce what is universal and abstract. Particular things or events cause only other particular things or events. It seems, therefore, that epiphenomenalism is no more compatible with the predicable relations in logic than are either identity materialism, idealism or standard dualism.

Nevertheless, it will be objected that our thesis that the predicable relations exclude standard dualism and idealism in particular rests on an undefended realism. For our case assumes that Aquinas is right that genus, difference and species in logic reflect matter, form and composite respectively in reality. This realism opposes both nominalism and conceptualism. For under the latter views it is simply denied that the predicables answer to anything in the world. So to show that these predicable relations exclude idealism and standard dualism, our assumption of realism as opposed to either nominalism or conceptualism must be justified.

To spell out the objection, nominalists and conceptualists deny that genus and difference are grounded in matter and form in respectively. Nominalists deny in the first instance that there are abstract ideas at all, genera and difference included. If they are right, then the realist claim collapses. Genus and difference *in mente* do not reflect matter and form *in re* or for that matter anything else in reality. For their part, conceptualists admit abstract ideas like genera and difference but deny that they are built on or reflect anything real. Classification in terms of them is instead wholly the work of minds. Accordingly, genus, difference, and species signify appearance and not reality, i.e. how we conveniently construe things for our own purposes and not how things really are.

In the scientific revolution at the time of Galileo, a quantitative view of the world replaced Aristotle's qualitative one. Under this change, only those features of a thing are real which are measurable. The rest supervene on the measurable together with perceiving subjects and belong to appearance. Based on quality and not quantity, then, genus, difference, and species just reflect the way we human beings view or organize reality and not reality itself. But if so, then from the genus-difference dichotomy in logic one falsely infers the matter-form complex in reality. And in that case no one successfully deduces simple or primal matter from the idea of the widest genus, form from difference or the composite of form and matter from species.

This harbors a kernel of truth. And that is that classification, along with the predicables of genus, difference and species that figure in it, are the work of mind. Like syllogisms and judgments, they are not real beings but that type of *entia rationis* which some scholastics called second intentions. Yet a glaring irony accompanies the objection. For the idea that science necessarily reveals the real world is one which science itself has long since abandoned. Consistent with Kant's "Copernican revolution" in epistemology, scientists have insisted for the past century or so that science does not reveal the world as it is in itself but the world only insofar as it can be made intelligible to us at a given stage of scientific opinion. So science too, it seems, is about appearance and not about reality. But in that case, the conceptualists' objection to a realist construal of the genus-difference schema is compromised. For then the option looms large that it is our genus-difference schema that mirrors reality and science that mirrors appearance, and not the other way around.

More fundamentally, though, modern conceptualism, to the extent that it follows Kant's transcendental move, has troubles of its own.. For as R.F.A. Hoernle has shown, to the question, "Can mind know its own constitution as knower'? Kantians can give no answer.[9] Mind must be able to do this for Kant. Otherwise it is not the aim of the *Critique of Pure Reason* to reveal the make-up of the knowing mind, i.e. as consisting of *a priori* categories on which *a priori* judgments are based. However, is the mind that is thus known, i.e. mind as knower, appearance or reality? The answer is that Kant can say neither one. Mind as knower does not belong to appearance since it is devoid of sense data. And since, for Kant, the real is unknown, then the same mind that Kant describes in his *Critique* cannot be real mind either. Hence, being neither phenomenal nor real, this same mind has no place in Kant's own scheme of things.

This line of argument can be put differently. If mind colors its objects, then when mind's object is mind, then mind colors mind. That means that in the core claim of Kantianism, i.e. "Mind colors its objects" the subject-term 'Mind' can only refer to phenomenal and not to real mind. But then Kantians cannot say after all that mind really does color its objects. For all they know, mind as it is in itself or real mind does not color its objects but is a *tabula rasa*, receiving things just as they are. And then their message comes to nothing. Nor can they really say that 'mind' here does refer to phenomenal mind. For what in the view of Kant colors its objects is transcendental mind, and the latter, having no empirical content, does not belong to phenomena at all. So the irony is that in the basal tenet of Kantianism, i.e. "Mind colors its objects" 'mind' has no suitable referent. It thus turns out in that program to be meaningless. To answer this, Kantians might concede that the judgment, "Mind colors its objects" is unmeaning. All intelligible judgments are about phenomena. However, so far from being phenomenal, mind is instead (along with things-in-themselves) the condition of the phenomenal, according to Kant. And what is a condition of the phenomenal evidently does not belong to the phenomenal it conditions.

Yet this reply is unavailable to Kantian conceptualists. If instead of belonging to phenomena mind is the condition of it, then mind is unknowable. But in that case the entire Kantian program collapses. As N.P. Stallknecht once put it,

> ....Once we call mind unknowable, along with the thing-in-itself, we must admit that space, time, and the categories need no longer be recognized as necessary characters of our mode of awareness, for we cannot determine what is necessary to something unknowable. And with that admission Kant's system crumbles.[10]

Nominalism, which denies abstract ideas, is no less self-defeating. The notion of an abstract idea figures in the disclaimer, "There are no abstract ideas." Yet that notion is evidently neither a sense image nor a copy thereof. It is neither particular nor concrete but universal and abstract. Thus do nominalists admit at least one abstract idea, i.e. the idea of an abstract idea, in their very denial of abstract ideas. They must then find a way of dissenting from abstract ideas without denying that there are abstract ideas. This, though, proves to be an impossible task. For just as one's believing that P implies one's judging that P, so too does one's disbelieving that P imply one's denying that P.

Besides, that there must be abstract ideas and hence that nominalism is false is shown by the irreducibility of subjects to predicates in subject-predicate propositions like 'Socrates is wise.' The expression, '...is wise' is a predicate but the expression '...is Socrates' cannot be a predicate. The reason is that subjects are logically proper names and as such they cannot be said of many. But any predicate can be said of many. If, therefore, '... is F' *can* be said of many (such as '...is wise') that can only be the case if '...is F' does not include in its sense the individuality of any individual F-thing. However, to say that '...is F' does not include in its sense any individual F-thing is just to say that '...is F' abstracts from the individuality of any individual F-thing, and so is an abstract idea. Therefore, it is a condition of the irreducibility of logical subjects to predicates in simple or subject-predicate propositions like 'Socrates is wise' that predicates are abstract ideas.

Suppose, then, that for the reasons given realism as regards the predicables gains support as over against either nominalism or conceptualism. In other words, suppose not only that there are abstract ideas but that they answer to something in reality. Then not only do the predicable relations exclude accounts of the person like identity materialism, standard dualism, epiphenomenalism and idealism but they also support the hylomorphic view that a person is a composite of soul and body and that the two are related to each other not as two complete substances in their own right but as form to matter in a single substance.

II

Nevertheless, though the foregoing account of the predicables suggests that the soul is the substantial form of the body and hence neither a body, supervenient on a body, nor a complete substance in its own right, it does not show the soul's independence of the body. On the contrary, it suggests that the soul depends on the body to exist since form (in the Aristotelian sense) must be the form of matter. And from this essential incompleteness of the soul, it seems to follow that the soul cannot exist without matter or the body. Yet for Aquinas not only is the soul the form of the body, but also and paradoxically, it is existentially independent of the body. And so the question is how Aquinas can have it both ways. How can the soul be so close to the body as to be its very substantial form and yet be existentially independent of the body?

The strongest argument for the latter, states Aquinas in *On Being and Essence*, is the soul's power of understanding. Forms, he there says, are understood or are actually intelligible only when "they are separated from matter and material conditions."[11] By 'matter' here it is meant prime matter and by 'material conditions' it is meant the conditions of concreteness and individuality. This separation occurs only through the power of an intelligent substance. When, for example, we know some form F, F extends to or is predicable of many particulars. But if in such knowledge F is received in our intellects as in matter, then F would be restricted to but one particular thing. For matter limits any form F to this or that F. Hence, our knowing F is not a case of F's being received in a material passivity.[12] The fact that the forms we know extend to or are predicable of various individuals is incompatible with their being received in our intellects as in matter. In other words, the character of universality or of being predicable of many that forms have as a result of their being in the passive intellect is inconsistent with a form's being in matter. Aquinas's argument is conveniently outlined as follows:

1. We understand some form F if and only if F is actually and not just potentially intelligible.
2. F is actually intelligible if and only if F is the form of the passive intellect.
3. It is a condition of F's being the form of the passive intellect that F is separated from matter and material conditions.
4. Hence, we understand some form F if and only if (i) F is the form of the passive intellect and (ii) F is to that extent separated from matter and material conditions.
5. If our passive intellect is either a body or the form of a body, then it is not the case both that F is the form of the passive intellect and that F is separated from matter and material conditions.
6. But it is evident that we do understand some form F.
7. Therefore, the passive intellect is neither a body nor the form of a body.

As for 1. and 2., intellect goes from potentially knowing F to actually knowing F and this implies that, with respect to F, intellect is passive.[13] This passivity of intellect with respect to F consists in its capacity to receive or be actualized by F. Just as in natural change matter receives or is actualized by form, so in knowing does the passive intellect receive or come to be actualized by form. In each case is the potentiality in question, i.e. matter and passive intellect, formless. As matter in natural change is pure potentiality for form, so in noetic change is intellect a blank tablet "on which nothing is written."[14]

Yet the two potentialities are different. Otherwise either matter is cognizant of the forms it receives or the possible intellect is not cognizant of the forms it receives. Says Aquinas,

> Then, too, prime matter is not cognizant of the forms which it receives. If, then, the receptivity of the possible intellect were the same as that of prime matter, the cognizant intellect would not be cognizant of the forms received. And this is false.[15]

This leads us to 3. When matter is actualized by the form F, the result is an F-thing, something that is naturally or physically F. But when the passive intellect receives the form F, no such result occurs. The passive intellect does not become an F-thing in receiving or in being actualized by the form F. Thus, when matter receives the form of feline, the result is a feline thing, i.e. a particular cat. For matter to receive the form of feline is for a particular cat to come to be. But when the passive intellect receives or is actualized by the form of feline, no particular cat is produced. The passive intellect does not become a cat in knowing what a cat is in and through receiving the form of feline. Nor, for its part, does matter know what a cat is in and through receiving the form of feline. Contrasting the receptivity of matter with that of both sense and intellect on this score Aquinas writes:

> Now, immutation is of two kinds, one natural, the other spiritual. Natural immutation takes place when the form of that which causes the immutation is received, according to its natural being, into the thing immuted, as heat is received into the thing heated. But spiritual immutation takes place when the form of what causes the immutation is received, according to a spiritual mode of being, into the thing immuted, as the form of color is received into the pupil which does not thereby become colored.[16]

What is meant by saying that F is received in matter according to a natural mode of being while F is received in both sense and intellect according to a spiritual mode of being? Aquinas' answer is that 'receiving a form F according to a spiritual mode of being' has two senses. Either F is received as separated from both matter and material conditions or F is received as separated from matter but not from material conditions. Sense knowledge receives its forms spiritually in the second sense while intellectual knowledge receives its form spiritually in the first sense. Because the sense of sight does not physically become green in receiving the particular green it sees, it is not a material potentiality or matter. Green here is not received in matter. That is what is meant by saying that it receives green as separated from matter. This is the second sense of receiving a form spiritually. In this same sense, the sense powers of animals as well as humans receive forms spiritually. Even so, the sense of sight does not receive green apart from material conditions. For the green it receives is always concrete and particular and never abstract and universal. And since concreteness and particularity are due to matter which limits any form F to this or that instance of F, it follows that green as well as all other sense objects are not received apart from material conditions, even though they are received apart from matter. That is why the sense powers do not receive their objects spiritually in the first sense.

Like the sense powers, the passive intellect too does not physically become the form it receives. My intellect does not become a cat in knowing cat any more than my sense of sight becomes green in seeing green. Forms are no more received in matter when they are received in intellect than they are received in matter when they are received in sense. But unlike the sense of sight and all other senses, the intellect receives its forms apart from material conditions in addition to receiving them apart from matter. Otherwise the objects of intellect would, like the objects of sense, be particular and concrete. But as it is, they are the very opposite. What I understand is understood universally and abstractly. Therefore, it can be said (as in 3 above) that it is a condition of my passive intellect's receiving some form F that F is separated both from matter and from material conditions.

That elicits two questions which take us to 5. First, what explains the fact that sense powers receive their objects spiritually in the second sense? Second, what explains the fact that the intellectual power receives its forms spiritually in the first sense? As to the first question, Aquinas answers that the explanation of this is that the sense power is neither prime matter nor a body. Otherwise in sense knowledge the various sense powers would physically become the forms which they receive. Yet, because sense objects are always received under material conditions (i.e. are concrete and particular) their respective sense powers, though neither matter nor a body, are nonetheless intimately connected with a body. For any sense power is the very form or act of a bodily organ. Sight, for example, is the form of the eye. It is this close association of sight with the eye that explains the concreteness and particularity that characterizes the objects of sight. The same goes for the other senses.

That suggests an answer to the second question. For Aquinas infers from this that since the objects of the intellectual power are not concrete and particular but abstract and universal instead, then that power is not the form of a bodily organ. In that sense is it a separated power, i.e. separate from a bodily organ. Spelled out the argument is this: If a cognitive power is the form of an organ, then the objects of that power are concrete and particular. But the objects of understanding are not concrete and particular but abstract and universal. It follows that the intellectual power in us is neither a body nor even the form or act of a body.[17]

To summarize the argument, the species of things are known only if "the intellect in act and the intelligible in act are one,"[18] i.e. only if it is those species themselves and not some copy of them are in the intellect. But a condition of a species being in the passive intellect is that it be abstracted from matter and material conditions. For things are received according to the mode of the receiver and the intellect receives things abstractly. But it is in turn a condition of this abstract mode of reception that the passive intellect is immaterial. It follows that the species of things are known only if the passive intellect is immaterial.[19]

So it is in the view of Aquinas that any object of knowledge is proportionate to its power.[20] The more dependent a power is on matter the more dependent on matter is its object. In the order of being, a power's status determines the status of its objects. Therefore, in the order of knowledge, one can deduce the status of a power from the status of its objects. Since, then, i) sense objects are individual while the objects of intellect are universal and ii) matter is the principle of individuality, then the sense power must be more dependent on the body than the intellectual power. But since for the reasons given, forms are not in *either* power received in matter, some other difference between the two powers as regards their relation to matter explains the difference between their respective objects. That difference in the view of Aquinas, is that a sense power, though not a body, is none the less the act of a bodily organ, whereas the intellectual power is neither a body nor even the act of a bodily organ.

That the intellectual power is not the act of an organ does not imply that the soul whose power it is is not the form of the body. Otherwise it is assumed that a soul has the same status in relation to matter as does its distinctive power. But that not only is not obvious but it is also untrue. The soul, says Aquinas, *is* the form of the body even though, paradoxically, its intellectual power is not the form of a bodily organ.

For this hylomorphic assay of soul and body, Aquinas gives indirect proofs. If Socrates say, is composed of soul and body as two complete substances, then Socrates is a mere aggregate and not one unqualifiedly speaking.[21] Not just that, but if what unites these two substances is another substance, then a further link is required to link the latter to what it links, and so on, *ad infinitum*?[22] To avoid all this, one might, with Plato, identify Socrates with his intellectual soul. That implies that Socrates' body is accidental to Socrates. But in that case, propositions like "Humans are animals" and "Humans are sentient beings" are accidental and not essential predications.[23] Besides, if Socrates' body is accidental to Socrates and no one senses without a body, then it is not one and the same person, Socrates, who is conscious both that he understands and that he senses.[24]

Of the direct proofs, one turns on the idea that difference is derived from the form.[25] To spell it out, though the intellect is not a body, body is nonetheless essential to what a person is. For the definition of a human being includes animal and the definition of animal includes body. If body is accidental to a person, then animal is not the genus of human.[26] But the definition of a human being includes rational as well as animal. For the distinctive, fundamental operation of a species is not accidental to it but belongs to its definition, and understanding is the distinctive, fundamental operation of humans. If understanding is accidental to a person, then rational is not the *differentia* of human. So the principle of understanding in humans, i.e. the intellectual soul, is part of what it is to be human. But it is evidently not the part from which genus is taken. For genus is taken from matter, and we saw that something excludes matter to the extent that it is intellectual. Unlike genus, difference or distinctiveness comes not from matter but from form.[27] It follows that the intellectual soul in a person is related to that person as his or her substantial form.

A second turns on the idea that a body is living by virtue of being *such* a body and not by virtue of being a body.[28] Otherwise all bodies are alive. But that a body is such a body is due to its form and not to its matter. Otherwise, since all bodies are composed of matter, all bodies are of the same sort. And then the very idea of being such a body as opposed to being another body is senseless. But the soul is defined as that by virtue of which a body is such a body, i.e. a living body. It follows that the soul is the form of any living body and hence the form of the human body.

Having reviewed what occasions the paradox, I return to the paradox itself. Does Aquinas recognize the enigma of saying that the soul is both form of the body and independent of the body? And if he does, does he try to show how those two theses are, and can be seen to be, compatible?

That St. Thomas recognizes the paradox is shown by his raising the objection that the soul's status as form of the body is incompatible with the immateriality of the soul's intellectual operation and power. But, so the objection runs, since the latter has already been shown, it follows that the soul is not the form of the body. Thus,

> Again, a thing's having its being in common with a body must have its operation in common with a body, for every thing acts in keeping with its being. Nor can the operative power of a thing be superior to its essence, since power is consequent upon principles of the essence of a thing. Now, if an intellectual substance is the form of a body, its being must be common to it and the body.... Therefore, an intellectual substance not only will have its operation in common with the body, but also its power will be a power in a body — a conclusion evidently impossible in the light of what has already been said.[29]

This objection (call it O) is conveniently summarized as follows:

(O)

1. Suppose that the soul is the form of the body.
2. Then the soul's being is common to it and the body.
3. But the operative powers of a thing follow its being.
4. So the soul's operative powers are common to it and the body.
5. But if so, then the soul's operative powers are in the body.
6. But it has been shown that the intellectual power of the soul is not in the body.
7. Therefore, 1 is false and the soul is not the form of the body.

To answer this objection is to explain the paradox in question. It is to show how the soul can be both the form of the body and yet independent of the body. In terms of (O), Aquinas denies that 2. follows from 1. Going by Aristotle's principle that activity follows being, Aquinas holds that we can infer how something is (exists) from knowing how its activity is. So if intellectual activity is intrinsically independent of matter then so too is the intellectual soul which is the subject of that activity. But at least simple apprehension or understanding the forms or essences of material things is an intellectual activity that is intrinsically independent of the body. It follows that the passive intellect which is actuated by those same forms or essences is also intrinsically independent of matter.

At *Summa contra gentiles*, chapter 69, no. 5–6, Aquinas fields the objection by denying the assumption on which it thrives. And that is that every power is consequent upon essence. In terms of (O), Aquinas denies that 2. follows from 1. He would also deny that (O)3 is necessarily true. If (O), 3. is false then (O), 7. is compromised and (O) fails. 'Being' in (O), 3. (as in (O), 1.) has the sense of essence. Yet, a soul's operative power need not follow the soul's being in the sense of its essence. It might follow its being in the sense of its *esse* or act of existence. What (O), 3. states, then, is not necessarily true of all powers of the soul. This reply hangs on Aquinas's celebrated distinction of essence and existence. It also turns on distinguishing the power of the soul from its essence, with the result that the former need not follow the latter.

What with these distinctions in place, then, (O) goes by the board. For then it does not follow, as (O) assumes, that *every* power of the soul is common to it and the body just because the soul's essence, as form of the body, is common to the soul and the body. For some powers might follow upon the soul's existence and not on its essence. And these powers would escape being in the body just in case the soul's act of existence is independent of the body. But that the soul's act of existence *is* independent of the body is shown by the fact that understanding is, for the reasons given, separate both from matter and material conditions. Since that implies that the intellectual power is not in a body and since any power that comes from the soul's essence *is* in a body (since body is included in the species human) it follows that the intellectual power is consequent on the soul's act of existence and not on its essence. Thus,

> Concerning the fifth argument, let it be said that because the soul is in its substance (essence) the form of the body, it does not follow that every operation of the soul must be performed by means of the body, so that every power of the soul will be the act of a bodily thing.... (the soul) can produce an operation without the body, as being operationally independent of the body; since it is neither *existentially* dependent on the body.[30]

Nevertheless, it might be objected that this Thomistic compromise fractures persons, splitting them in two. It is as if a person's essence goes one way and a person's existence goes another. Persons depend on matter so far as their essence is concerned but they do not depend on matter so far as their existence is concerned. True, drawing this distinction *prima facie* skirts the contradiction that persons in the same respect both do and do not depend on matter. But does it really escape the contradiction? If matter enters into a thing's definition, then is it possible that that same thing exists independently of matter? Is that not like saying that though the concept *animal* enters into the concept *dog*, there can nonetheless be non-animal dogs?

This last question Aquinas would answer in the negative. True, if a predicate P enters as a constituent part of the definition of a subject S, it is impossible that S exists without P. Therefore, since matter or body enters as a constituent part into the definition of a person, it follows that no person ever is or exists without a body.

Even so, what holds for persons need not hold for the souls of persons. And eschewing Platonism, Aquinas denies that persons are identified with their souls. True, persons can neither be defined nor can they exist without matter. In this they are just like anything else whose essence is a composite of matter and form. With respect to all such things, one cannot say that their existence runs contrary to their concepts. If their concepts or essences include matter as a constituent part then there is no question of their existing independently of matter. Yet unlike a person's essence, the soul's essence does not comprise both matter and form as constituent parts but is form alone. Any soul, the souls of brutes included, has a simple and not a composite essence. Being form alone and not a composite of form and matter, then, no soul as soul includes matter as a constituent part of its definition. But if that is so, then it is no contradiction in terms after all to say that the soul can exist without matter.

To this it might be countered that Aquinas avoids the contradiction in this way only by surrendering his belief that the soul depends on matter for its concept or essence. True, if matter does not in the first instance enter into the concept of the soul as one of its constituent parts, then Aquinas cannot be charged with a contradiction in terms in affirming that the soul does not depend on matter to exist. But the trouble is that to embrace the antecedent here seems to imply that the soul is independent of matter in concept as well as in existence.

To this counter-objection, though, I think that Aquinas would reply by distinguishing two ways in which the definition of one concept depends on another concept.[31] One can say that one concept depends on another either intrinsically or extrinsically. To say that the definition of a concept *c* intrinsically depends on another concept *d* is to say that *d* is a constituent part of the definition of *c*. Thus, the concept stone depends on body because the concept of body is the genus of stone. When a concept depends on another concept in this way, it is evidently a contradiction in terms to affirm that any instance of *c* exists or can exist independently of *d*. A stone is inconsistently said to be incorporeal. However, to say that the definition of a concept *c* extrinsically depends on another concept *d* is to say that one cannot define *c* without adverting to something (*d*) that, so far from its being a constituent part of *c*, is utterly opposed and alien to *c*. Thus, one cannot define the concept of actuality without bringing in the opposed notion of potentiality. In a loose sense, one can say that potentiality enters into the definition of actuality. But it does not enter into it as one of its constituent parts. Otherwise the contradiction ensues that the actual is the potential. As it is with actuality and potentiality, so is it with the concepts of form and matter. You cannot define form without bringing in the notion of matter. Yet, matter is not a constituent part of form. Otherwise form would be matter.

Suppose, then, that it is conceded that a soul is a certain form, i.e. the substantial form of a body. Then the concept of body cannot enter into the concept of the soul as one of its constituent parts any more than matter can in this way enter into the concept of any other form. Otherwise the soul would be body and not the form of a body. All the same, the concept of soul does in a sense conceptually depend on the concept of body just as any form conceptually depends on matter. To say this is to say that, taken in and of itself soul has an incomplete essence, the incompleteness being completed by the concept of body. But because its completion by body is a completion by something that is both opposed and logically posterior to it, it is not contradictory to say that the soul can exist without body. It is no more contradictory to say this than it is to say that form can exist without matter, actuality can exist without potentiality, or substance can exist without accident. And this is so for the same reason. For here again, matter, potentiality, and accident are both opposed and logically posterior to form, actuality, and substance, respectively.

Quite generally, then, one can say that whenever one concept c extrinsically depends on another concept d such that d is both opposed to and logically posterior to c, then one consistently says that c can exist independently of d. So even though concepts like form, actuality, and soul conceptually depend on the opposite notions of matter, potentiality and body, respectively, there need not be existential dependence of the former on the latter. True, we cannot define form, actuality, and soul without adverting to the concepts of matter, potentiality, and body, respectively. Still, that this conceptual dependence is extrinsic and not intrinsic and that the latter are logically posterior to the former imply that one consistently says that form, actuality, and soul can exist independently of matter, potentiality and body, respectively.

In summary: that Aquinas's view of the soul is paradoxical no one can deny. But paradox is not contradiction. One compatibly says both that the soul is the form of the body and that it is independent of the body. It all depends on what in this context it is meant by 'independent.' For the reasons given, Aquinas denies that form necessarily depends on matter existentially just because it depends on matter essentially or for its definition.[32] Further, he affirms that it is possible that the soul's powers follow its being in the sense of its existence as well as its essence. That this possibility is in fact actualized is shown by the fact of human understanding. If the status of a power is shown by its act and if actual understanding is independent of matter then so too is the power of understanding from which it springs. That same power, therefore, must follow on the soul's existence and not its essence. For since matter enters into the human essence, powers that flow from the latter are not independent of matter. Their subject is not the soul alone but the composite of soul and body. If, then, i) power follows being, ii) the power of understanding is independent of matter and material conditions, and iii) a person's being in the sense of essence includes matter, then the paradox in question follows. While the soul's being in the sense of essence depends on matter in the sense specified, the soul's being in the sense of its existence is nonetheless subsistent or independent of matter.

NOTES

1. St. Thomas Aquinas, *Summa theologica*, I, q 76, a. 1, in A. Pegis, ed., *Introduction to St. Thomas Aquinas* (New York: The Modern Library, 1948), 291–97.

2. For a detailed account of these functions of judgment, see H. B. Veatch, *Intentional Logic* (New Haven: Yale University Press, 1952), 164–69. See also, R.W. Schmidt, *The Domain of Logic According to Saint Thomas Aquinas* (The Hague: Martinus Nijhoff, 1966), 209–212.

3. For an account of the difference between abstraction and precision and of how the former allows whereas the latter excludes predication, see St. Thomas Aquinas, *On Being and Essence*, trans. A. Maurer (Toronto: Pontifical Institute of Medieval Studies, 1949), Chapter II, 33–38.

4. Ibid., *On Being and Essence*, trans. A. Maurer, Chapter II, 33–38.

5. Plato, *Phaedo*, in B. Jowett, trans., *The Dialogues of Plato* (Oxford: The Clarendon Press, 1953) 103b 5, 461.

6. The widest genus is simple and not a composite of genus and difference. Otherwise it is not the widest genus. Compare Wittgenstein's argument that there must be simple objects if factual propositions are to have precise sense. See L. Wittgenstein, *Tractatus Philosophicus*, trans. Pears and McGuinness (London: Routledge & Kegan Paul, 1961), 2.02 –2.0211. For a lucid discussion and interpretation of Wittgenstein's argument, see David Pears, *The False Prison: A Study of the Development of Wittgenstein's Mind* (Oxford: The Clarendon Press, 1987), Chapter 4. See also, David Pears, *Ludwig Wittgenstein* (New York: The Viking Press, 1970), 57–65.

7. St. Thomas Aquinas, *On Being and Essence*, trans. A. Maurer, Chapter II, 34–35.

8. Ibid., *On Being and Essence*, trans. A. Maurer, Chapter II, 35–36.

9. R.F.A. Hoernle, review of H. J. Paton, *Kant's Metaphysic of Experience*, in Mind, n.s., Vol. XLVI, (1937), 500–02.

10. N.P. Stallknecht and R. Brumbaugh, *The Spirit of Western Philosophy* (New York: David McKay Co., Inc., 1964), 381.

11. St. Thomas Aquinas, *On Being and Essence*, trans. A. Maurer, Chapter IV, 43.

12. St. Thomas Aquinas, *Summa theologica*, trans. A. Pegis, I, q. 84, a. 2, 380-382.

13. Ibid., *Summa theologica*, trans. A. Pegis, I, q. 79, a. 2, 338-340.

14. Ibid., *Summa theologica*, trans. A. Pegis, I, q. 79, a. 2, 338-340.

15. St. Thomas Aquinas, *Summa contra gentiles*, trans. James F. Anderson (Notre Dame, IN., Univ. of Notre Dame Press, 1975), Book II, chapter 59, no. 5, 178.

16. St. Thomas Aquinas, *Summa theologica*, trans. A. Pegis, I, q. 78, a. 3, 327–329.

17. Ibid., *Summa theologica*, trans. A. Pegis, I, q. 85, a. 1, 400–407.

18. St. Thomas Aquinas, *Summa contra gentiles*, trans. James F. Anderson, Book II, chapter 59, no.13, 180; See also Aristotle, *De anima*, III, 4 (430a 3).
19. Ibid., *Summa contra gentiles,* trans. James F. Anderson, Book II, chapter 50, no. 3, 149.
20. St. Thomas Aquinas, *Summa theologica,* trans. A. Pegis, I, q. 85, a. 1, 400–407.
21. St. Thomas Aquinas, *Summa contra gentiles*, trans. Jams F. Anderson, Book II, chapter 57, no. 3, 169.
22. Ibid., *Summa contra gentiles,* trans. James F. Anderson, Book II, chapter 58, no. 8, 175.
23. Ibid., *Summa contra gentiles*, trans. James F. Anderson, Book II, chapter 58, no. 7, 175.
24. St. Thomas Aquinas, *Summa theologica,* trans. A. Pegis I, q. 76, a. 1, 291-297.
25. Ibid., *Summa theologica,* trans. A. Pegis I, q. 76, a. 1, 291-297.
26. Ibid., *Summa theologica,* trans. A. Pegis I, q. 76, a. 3, 302-306.
27. St.Thomas Aquinas, *On Being and Essence*, trans. A. Maurer, Chapter II, 35.
28. St. Thomas Aquinas, *Summa theologica,* trans. A. Pegis I, q. 75, a. 1, 281-283.
29. St. Thomas Aquinas, *Summa contra gentiles,* trans. James F. Anderson, Book II, chapter 56, no. 18, 168.
30. Ibid. *Summa contra gentiles*, trans. James F. Anderson, Book II, chapter 69, no. 6, 208 (parentheses and italics are mine).
31. St.Thomas Aquinas, *On Being and Essence*, trans. A. Maurer, Chapter VI, 55.
32. Ibid., *On Being and Essence*, trans. A. Maurer, Chapter IV, 44.

Chapter Six

Ethics

St. Thomas's ethics is a type of natural-law ethics. Like Aristotle, Aquinas viewed ethics as a science and hence as a body of knowledge which proceeds from first principles. The latter include the idea of good, the basic concept of ethics, just as first principles in metaphysics include the idea of being, the basic concept in metaphysics. Thus, as the first principle in metaphysics is that something cannot both be and not be at the same time in the same respect, so the first principle in ethics is that one ought to do good and avoid evil.[1] Now for Aquinas as for Aristotle, 'good' has the nature of an end.[2] So Aquinas' first principle of ethics comes down to this: One ought to do that which conduces to one's end as a human being, and avoid what deters or is inconsistent with one's reaching that end. In any case, believing as he did in the self-evident status of ultimate ethical principles, Aquinas would oppose as strongly as did Plato and Aristotle the views of moral skepticism and moral relativism. One unacceptable consequence of the latter is that no one can say that objectively speaking anything was any better than anything else. You could not say that, objectively speaking, kindness is better than cruelty, that justice is any better than injustice, or that tolerance is better than intolerance. Rejecting this consequence, Aquinas would deny the relativism which implies it.

That aside, though Aquinas' ethics is to a large extent Aristotelian, it none the less adds a religious dimension to the *Nicomachean Ethics*. For Aquinas is a Christian philosopher and Aristotle pre-dates Christianity. That makes for a difference between them as regards their approach to ethics. Perhaps the most important difference centers on the identity of the final end or *summum bonum* of persons. The ethics of both philosophers are teleological and eudemonistic. Right actions are those that are conducive to a certain end and that end is happiness.[3] Yet they differ as to what happiness consists in. For

Aristotle it is acting and thinking well in this life just as a human being.[4] But for Aquinas the *summum bonum* is identified with something transcendent to which virtue in this life is directed as means. That is the vision of God in the next life, the Beatific Vision.[5] In what follows I focus first on the Aristotelian influence on Aquinas's ethics. Then I consider those aspects of his ethics in which Aquinas either departs or goes beyond Aristotle.

However, to recur to the idea of natural law, just what is the central premise of an ethics that is based on that notion? In a word, it is this: that anything at all ought to operate or act in accord with its natural purpose or end. To see what this comes to, consider the following dialogues:

A: This saw is not doing what it ought to do.

B: Why?

A: Because its purpose is to cut and it's not doing that, i.e. not operating in conformity with its purpose.

A: Jones is not doing what he ought to do as physician.

B: Why?

A: Because Jones' purpose as a physician is to heal and he's not doing that, i.e. not acting in accordance with his purpose as physician.

A: Smith is not doing what he ought to do as a person.

B: Why?

A: Because Smith's purpose just as a person is to think and act rationally and he is not doing that, i.e. not acting in accordance with his purpose as a person.

The argument behind these three exchanges is:

> Anything that does what it ought to do acts or operates in accordance with its purpose.
> x is not acting or operating in accordance with its purpose.
> Therefore, x is not doing what x ought to do.

Here, as is evident, 'ought' is defined in terms of 'conformity to purpose or end,' the latter being the norm or standard of correct or right action or operation. And since good has the nature of an end, 'ought' is therefore defined in terms of 'good.' Thus,

> Anything ought to operate or act how it is good for it to operate or act.

Hence, any person s taken as person ought to act how it is good for s to act as a person.

But the good of anything is identified with its end.

Therefore, any person s taken as a person ought to act according to s's end as a person.

In summary: when we use a saw and say that it is not doing what it ought to do and someone asks why, we respond that it is not accomplishing its purpose as a saw. Here, 'ought' is defined in terms of end. Again, when we say that incompetent physicians are not doing what they ought to do, and someone asks why, we reply that their actions flout their end as physicians which is to heal. It is the same with persons who are not doing what they ought to do not as physicians but as persons. Their actions tragically fly in the face of their very own natural end as persons. This is the core idea in natural law ethics.

Stated differently, the concept of natural law ethics might be summarized as follows:

1. Anything ought to do what it is good for it to do.
2. A thing's doing what it is inclined by its specific difference to do is its doing what it is good for it to do. For that activity is its end, and the good of a thing is its end. For example, the specific difference of a carpenter is wood-building since a carpenter is defined as the wood-building artisan. Hence, the end and good of a carpenter is building with wood since that activity conforms to and reflects his specific difference.
3. Hence, anything ought to do what it is inclined by its specific difference to do.
4. Therefore, persons ought to do what they are inclined by their specific difference to do.
5. But being rational animals, persons are inclined by their specific difference to act rationally.
6. Therefore, a person ought to act and live rationally or according to reason.

We saw previously that it is not only persons but other living things as well that have natural ends.[6] Immanent activities occur in living things, humans included, that are regularly followed by the same results. Thus, reproductive changes regularly occur in adult paramecia before they begin to split. The fact that activities like these occur regularly and across the board in all living things is due neither to chance nor to absolute necessity.[7] The former fails to cover the regularity of the occurrences and the latter fails to account for exceptions to the regularity. Moreover, for the reasons that were previously cited, it cannot be said that the cause of any such immanent change in an organism is either another such change or a change that begins in something else. What, then, is it? We saw that the only plausible answer is that these immanent changes are drawn out of an organism by a final cause or end which by definition pre-exists those changes and is in mind as opposed to matter.[8] This mind can only be a directing principle which knows the end of each thing and the means by which it is achieved.

This pattern of means to end in a thing is one thing that is meant by a thing's natural law.[9] However, the directing mind or God does not know the natural law of a thing because it is, but it is because God knows and wills it. Otherwise God's knowledge is determined by things. Otherwise too, the regularity with which these vital immanent changes are followed by the same results is not explained by a pre-existing mental end as was shown. Therefore, the natural law of each thing exists eternally in the divine Mind as the pre-existing plan of each thing.

But if this is true generally and across the board, then it is true in the case of persons. Immanent changes in us occur and are regularly followed by the same results. Since this is due neither to chance nor to brute necessity, and since these changes are not explained either by prior immanent changes or by changes that begin outside the agent, then they too are traced to a directing mind which ordains these same changes as means to an end.[10] In other words, they are traced to a mind which establishes the natural law of persons. And once again, this directing mind or God knows this natural law of persons not because it is but it is because God knows and wills it.

For example, suppose that by close and repeated observation I come to know what condors are. This simple apprehension is evidently an immanent change. The mental act whereby my active intellect focuses on the nature of a condor in the particular condors I sense taken apart from the individuating aspects of those condors both begins and ends in me. This mental act is called abstraction. In any case, it was previously shown that the full explanation of this immanent change is not another change, either immanent or transitive. It is an end or final cause to which my apprehension tends. This is the apprehended object, i.e. the form of a condor, which is instantiated in the particular condors I have sensed. To the extent that it is the form of a material thing, the form of a condor is the sort of thing to which my knowing power is naturally oriented. For being the forms of our bodies and not separated substances, our minds for that reason have as their objects forms in matter as opposed to separated forms.[11] That aside, this relation of orientation is none other than the relation of a thing to its end. The form of a condor then, as well as the forms of other things in the world, are the natural ends of our power of simple apprehension. For the latter is naturally oriented to becoming those forms intentionally.

Nevertheless, this form of a condor in particular condors is end with respect to our power of apprehension in a secondary and not in the primary sense. For we saw in chapter three that primarily speaking an end is in mind and not in matter.[12] Forms in matter are called ends only secondarily speaking, i.e. only because they mimic pre-existing ends in minds of which they are the results in matter. Thus, as finished product, the *Athene* mimics the pre-existing model of it in Phidias's mind of which it is the result in matter. We evidently call the latter end only because it exemplifies in matter what primarily is end, namely, the pre-existing model of it in mind. And as it is with artifacts like the *Athene*, so is it with natural things. The forms of particular condors are ends only by virtue of exemplifying in matter what is primarily speaking end, i.e. the model or exemplar of condor in God's mind. There, the form of condor is not joined to this other thing matter as it is in the world but it is the form of condor as such or *simpliciter*. As in individual condors the form of condor is form participatively speaking whereas in God it is form non-participatively speaking, so too the form of condor in individual condors is end participatively speaking whereas in God it is end non-participatively speaking. For something is end to the extent that it is actual with respect to some other thing which tends to it as what is potential tends to what is actual. Therefore, something that is a mix of form and matter or of the actual and the potential is not end as such but end only participatively speaking. It is end or good not just as such but end or good as joined to another thing, matter, in which it exists. For quite generally, if something is participatively speaking F, (i.e. if it is F as exemplified in matter) then it is called F only secondarily speaking, i.e. only on account of something else which is primarily or non-participatively speaking F. That is because what is participatively F is caused by what is non-participatively F. You cannot cite as the cause of what is participatively F — just insofar as it is participatively F — some other thing that is also participatively F. No explanation is or includes the thing explained without circularity.

So in an ultimate sense, the final cause of the immanent change which consists in my apprehending the nature or form of a condor is not that form in matter. The latter is more the efficient cause of that apprehension. Instead, it is that same form as Idea in God. As anything in the world is being only by virtue of what is Being in Itself, which is not in the world, so too any form in the world which is the end or good of something (as the form of condor in particular condors is an end or good in relation to my power of simple apprehension) is so only by virtue of goodness itself or end-in-itself which is not in the world. Says Aquinas,

> ...Everything is therefore called good from the divine goodness as from the first exemplary, effecting and final principle of all goodness. Nevertheless, everything is called good by reason of the likeness of the divine goodness

belonging to it, which is formally its own goodness, by which it is denominated good. And so of all things there is one goodness, and yet many goodnesses.[13]

Granted that this is so, several questions arise. Under what conditions do the actions of persons taken as persons flout their natural end as persons? When do those actions accord with that same end? And what evidence is there in the first instance that persons have a natural end just as persons? One way to answer these questions is to begin by distinguishing the theoretical and the practical sciences, showing that ethics belongs to the latter. Then, by comparing ethics with other practical sciences, the answers to the foregoing questions emerge.

THEORETICAL AND PRACTICAL SCIENCES

Like Aristotle Aquinas distinguished theoretical and practical sciences.[14] So the question becomes, "How does Aquinas classify ethics"? If science is defined as a body of knowledge that proceeds from first principles, then his answer is that ethics is a science. Included in the first principles of ethics are, "Good is objectively different from evil" and "One should do good and avoid evil."[15] These practical first principles match theoretical first principles in that we by nature believe and adhere to them. And for Aquinas ethics is a practical science since its goal is knowledge for the sake of action and not knowledge for its own sake. The purpose of ethics is not just to give us knowledge of right actions but to get us actually to act rightly.[16] By this measure, mathematics is a theoretical science and agriculture is a practical science. Agriculture is knowledge of how to produce food and ward of disease in plants. This knowledge is evidently not for its own sake but for the sake of growing crops. It is knowledge for the sake of practice. But mathematics is just knowledge of numbers and their relations. Though it is indispensable for many practical uses, it is not knowledge for the sake of doing something or action but knowledge for the sake of knowledge.[17]

However, in the practical sciences, the action aimed at is sometimes final end and sometimes not. When it is the former, the science is performative and when it is not, it is productive. Action in the latter is aimed at for the sake of some further end which is not action but the final end of action. Agriculture aims at food-producing activities. Yet it is evident that not these actions but food-production is the final end. Fertilizing, planting, reaping, etc. are the ends of the farmer, but the end of the farmer as engaged in these activities is food. Thus, the actions of fertilizing, planting, reaping, and so on all aim at something else, namely, food-production. Most practical sciences fall into this category. They are mixed and not pure practical sciences because the action aimed at is not the final but an intermediate end. Besides agriculture, these include shipbuilding, car-making, drug-making, and so on.

ETHICS AS FIRST PRACTICAL SCIENCE

Ethics is different. It aims at how one ought to be and act just as a human being. In that way it differs from most other practical sciences which aim not just at action but in the long run at some product of the action. Thus one might call ethics a performative and not a productive practical science.

Whether productive and performative, practical sciences are normative. Their end is fitting or appropriate action in some capacity. In productive sciences the action is not itself end but means to another end which is some non-action such as a product or state of affairs. Thus, the end of a person as having the art of agriculture is food-production. Here, persons do what they ought to do as farmers. And the action measures up to what it ought to be depending on whether or not it produces food. So in productive practical sciences the norm is some product or state of affairs. But in performative practical sciences the norm is some action. And this action itself is the end. In singing, emitting sounds in a certain way is the norm and end of a singer as singer. Likewise in ethics, habitually acting virtuously just as persons is the norm and end of actions.

Ethics is first practical science. Other practical sciences also aim at right action. But they do so in the non-moral sense of 'right.' There is right action in house-building, car-production and so on. Here, actions are right if and only if they tend to their respective ends, i.e. a house and a car. They are in all cases actions that strike a middle course between being too much and too little, i.e. erring neither on the side of excess nor on the side of defect. Instead, they are "just right" or follow what in the Aristotelian tradition is called right reason. House-builders fit doors into frames neither too tightly nor too loosely, and shipbuilders bend planks neither too much nor too little but just right. But ethics aims at how artisans and everyone else ought to act as persons. This is right action in the moral sense of being virtuous action. And it is also action that errs neither by excess nor by defect. Like fitting action in art and craft, virtuous action in ethics hits a mean between these extremes. Acting according to right reason, the just person steers a middle course between harshness and leniency.

As was said, all of this implies that ethics is first practical science. The reason is that all other practical sciences include the idea of a person's acting according to the mean. But ethics does not include the idea of acting according to the mean in house-building, car-making, dentistry, etc. Acting according to right reason as a person does not include acting according to right reason in house-building, car-making, etc. However, a person's acting according to right reason in these and all other practical skills *does* include that person's acting according to right reason. Good house-builders are not *ipso facto* good persons. However, in good house-building, good house-builders *ipso facto* follow the same principle that they would follow if they were acting as good persons, namely, acting according to right reason. The same relation holds between ethics and every other practical science. The latter include acting so as to strike the golden mean but the former does not include striking the golden mean in any one of the specialized ways in which the latter does. Since, then, other practical sciences include the rule of striking the mean but ethics does not include the special application of that rule which is peculiar to any one of the other practical sciences, it follows that ethics is regulative of the other practical sciences or in other words is the first or the most general practical science.

So it is that ethics is to the other practical sciences what metaphysics is to the other theoretical sciences. While the principles of being as being, the object of metaphysics, are included in the objects of all the other theoretical sciences, the latter are not included in the objects of metaphysics. That is why metaphysics is first among all theoretical sciences.

THE ETHICAL OBJECT

Yet exactly what is the object of ethics? If house-building studies how to construct houses and if car-making studies how best to produce cars, and so on, what does ethics study? This question is in a way misplaced. After all, these sciences are unlike ethics in being productive practical sciences. House-building and car-making aim at some product, i.e. a house and a car. These ends are outside and beyond the agents and the actions they use to reach those ends. This is not the case with ethics. Ethics evidently aims at something, but the latter is hardly some product or state that is external to the agent and his or her action. For ethics has to do with doing and not with making or producing. So to fit, the question should be this: if singing is about emitting certain sounds in a pleasant way and if dancing is about making certain movements with the body in a pleasing way, what is ethics about? Asking the question this way avoids two category mistakes, namely, mixing ethics with non-practical sciences such as biology and physics and mixing ethics with non-performative practical sciences like house-building and car-making. It is also on target in that ethics is a normative science just like the arts of singing and dancing. Yet, the analogy still limps since ethics is a science and the arts of singing and dancing are not. Moreover, ethics studies how one ought to act just as a person *period* and not necessarily as before an audience given the norms of song and dance of a certain culture. Thus ethics differs from the arts of singing and dancing.

To say that ethics is about acting rightly as persons implies a norm. Yet the ethical norm is not external like the ends of the productive practical sciences. It is not a house, a car, food, etc. To the question, "What is the ethical norm"? part of the answer is that the norm is internal and not external. Another part is that the ethical norm is a kind of acting or activity and not either a kind of making or a kind of product. With what is this activity identified?

THE ETHICAL NORM

The full answer is that the ethical norm is identified with acting rationally or according to right reason. However, since it was implied that this norm is also the natural end of persons, the objection might be raised as to whether persons have a natural end just as persons. For even if they have goals in incidental capacities, how does it follow that persons have a goal or end just as persons? This seems to be a *non-sequitur*.

Yet the objection oversimplfies the argument as the following outline of the argument shows. Practical as opposed to theoretical sciences are distinguished by their ends. Knowledge is the end of the latter whereas doing or acting is the end of the former. Therefore, being a practical science, ethics has action as its end. But the final end in ethics is acting and not some product or state which action produces. Moreover, the ethical end is not the action of someone as in a special and incidental capacity but the action of a person as person. Otherwise ethics aims at right action as house-builder, car-maker, etc. Therefore, 1) since ethics is evidently a practical science, 2), since agents in practical sciences have ends as possessing certain capacities, 3), since those ends are one with activities that are unique to those agents in those capacities, and 4), since ethics aims at right action just as being a person, then it follows 5), that persons have an end just as persons and that the latter is activity that is unique to persons as persons.

Acting well as persons is acting rationally. That is because persons are rational and not non-rational animals, and a thing acts fittingly or well just when its actions or activities conform to its nature. We say of an injured sparrow that it does not behave as it ought to behave. It has difficulty flying, its movements on the ground are unusual and erratic, either it cannot gather food or build a nest at all or it does so awkwardly and abnormally. By saying that it is not acting how it ought to act we mean that its actions fail to conform to its nature. Likewise, we say of persons who are acting irrationally that they are not acting how they ought to act. And once again this means that their actions flout their very nature as rational animals. By analogy, recall the examples which were previously given. If A is using a saw and says that it is not doing what it ought to do and B asks why, A responds that it is not accomplishing its purpose as a saw. Here, 'ought' is defined in terms of end. Again, if it is asked why physicians are said not to be acting as they ought to act when they make patients worse off instead of better off, the answer can only be that their actions flout their end as physicians which is to heal. It is the same with persons who are not doing what they ought to do not as physicians but as persons. Their actions fly in the face of their very own natural end as persons, i.e. to act according to right reason.

Moreover, rational action as opposed to rational thinking is rational by participation and not rational in itself. For the latter is thought and not action. As the former always includes the latter, the latter is logically prior to the former and related to the former as the simple to the composite. When I solve mathematical puzzles, I engage in activity that is rational in itself. But when in building I apply that knowledge in fitting beams at just the right angles, my action is rational by participation. My action includes activity that is rational in itself, i.e. mathematical reasoning, but adds to it something else, namely, putting that knowledge to work in constructing a building according to right reason. That is why this latter activity is rational by participation. Again, knowledge of physiology is rational in itself. But when, applying that knowledge, I exercise neither so little as to lose muscle tone nor so much as to risk injury, then my action is rational by participation. It is action that conforms to reason in that it hits the mean between excess and deficiency.

Along with all the other practical sciences, ethics is knowledge of activity that is rational by participation. It is knowledge for the sake of action. Knowing how to build a car leads car-builders to act in certain ways and to refrain from acting in other ways, given the end in view, namely, a car. And when they do act in these ways given the end in question, their actions accord with right reason. But when they act in ways that are not conducive to the end, i.e. when their actions err on the side of either excess or defect, then their actions are wrong actions or actions that flout right reason.

The aim in ethics is not a car and hence not acting according to right reason in car-building but rational living and acting just as a human being. Yet rational living and acting as a human being follows the same rule of acting in accord with right reason or steering a middle course between excess and defect. The aim is habitually to strike the mean of action in everyday living. And to the extent that we do this our actions are virtuous. Thus, the virtue of humility gets between boastfulness and self-debasement, the virtue of temperance shuns the extremes of indulgence and insensibility, the virtue of liberality falls between extravagance and stinginess, and so on.

It was said that action according to right reason is the ideal in arts and crafts just as it is the ideal action in persons as persons. It is that which makes the actions of crafts-persons good, just as it is that which makes the actions of persons as persons good. And since the idea of persons acting according to right reason is included in right action in the specialized crafts (house-building, medicine, etc.), but the idea of persons acting according to right reason in house-building, medicine, etc. is not included in the idea of persons acting according to right reason, it follows that ethics — which concerns persons acting according to right reason period — is prior and architectonic with respect to all of the other practical sciences. In short, while house-building, medicine or any other practical science always adds some *differentia* to the idea of practical science while ethics does not, ethics is practical science pure and simple. It is not one among other practical sciences as coordinate with or as on the same level as the others, but it is instead hierarchically first among all practical sciences, just as metaphysics is hierarchically first among all theoretical sciences.

THE OBJECTION OF NARROWNESS

Nevertheless, the foregoing conception of moral virtue as striking a mean between excess and defect is susceptible of an objection. And that is that it is too narrow to catch virtuous acts that are not a mean. Not every vice is either the excess or the deficiency of an action or feeling. Some vices, e.g. murder, perjury and adultery, are wrong in themselves and not wrong because the degree in which they are done is either deficient or excessive. And so by the same token, some virtues, say, telling the truth and keeping promises, are right in themselves and not right because they fall between excess and defect. As between virtue and vice there must be a complete parallelism since they are contraries and not contradictories. If a form of social injustice is correctly identified, then there is evidently a corresponding form of social justice. Either, therefore, it is wrong to confine virtuous action to a mean between both excess and defect or else acts like murder, perjury and the like are not wrong in themselves but wrong only because they are excessive or deficient actions. In other words, the objection is that the definition of virtue in terms of a mean is defensible only if no actions or feelings are right or wrong in themselves but become right or wrong according to how they are used by us. If they are used according to reason, then they are a mean and hence right; but if they are not used according to reason, then they are an excess or defect and hence wrong.

This problem impacts the identity-in-difference relation that was shown to obtain between ethics and the other practical sciences. If being a mean between undesirable extremes is the definition of moral virtue, then the hierarchical identity-in-difference relation of ethics to the other practical inquiries remains intact. For the identity side of that relation is preserved. Though it is preeminent among practical disciplines for the reasons previously given, ethics is in a sense identical with its subordinate family members. For they one and all of them concern acting according to right reason and this is action that is a mean between excess and defect. It is just that in ethics it is acting according to reason *period* while in the subordinate practical sciences it is acting according to reason in building, healing, farming, etc. Also, in ethics the action is end and not mere means while in the subordinate practical crafts the action is mere means.

However, if, to cover intrinsically vicious acts, morally virtuous acts are defined either as those that conform to a specific moral rule or those that are done for the sake of a moral rule, then the definition is too narrow to catch acts that are right because they strike a mean between extremes. And then the identity-in-difference tie between ethics and the other practical inquiries is ruined. And it is ruined because the identity side of the relation is lost. For acting virtuously is no longer defined as hitting the mean period, given conditions of human living, as skilled surgeons act in the right degree in surgery given the conditions of patients. For intrinsically vicious action is not vicious because it either exceeds or falls short of the degree or way in which it ought to be done. It is vicious just because of the kind of act it is.

The difficulty is conveniently framed in a dilemma. Either being a mean between excess and defect is or is not the definition of moral virtue. If it is, then, by parity of reasoning, being excessive or deficient action is the definition of vicious action. But then it follows that no account is given of intrinsically vicious acts. But if being a mean is not the definition of virtue and virtuous acts are defined instead as those that conform to a specific moral rule, then intrinsic virtue and vice are accounted for at the cost of cutting the tie between ethics and the other practical sciences. For then the identity side of the hierarchical identity-in-difference relation between ethics and the other practical inquiries is lost. Is it possible to escape the dilemma and have it both ways?

TOWARD A SOLUTION

The answer is to deny both that virtue is defined as being a mean in acting and that this implies severing the tie between ethics and its family members in the practical disciplines. One must first give a definition of moral virtue that is broad enough to cover both acts that are a mean between excess and defect and acts that are intrinsically good. Then one must show that under this broader definition the preeminent but integral place of ethics among practical inquiries remains intact. Such a definition, we shall find, incorporates the Thomistic idea of natural law as moral standard.

The first step is reached by defining morally virtuous action as the action of a person as person that accords with reason. This wider definition allows two kinds of vicious acts. These are: i) acts that are vicious because they flout reason by excess or defect and ii) acts that are vicious because they flout reason in principle. To the extent that the former, imprudent actions are done, the natural end of the actor is not removed. Here, the end might be reached but it is imperfectly reached. But to the extent that the latter are done, that same end is unrealizable. This more or less reflects the belief of common sense that some wrongs are faults and others crimes. The second phase of the solution is to show that under this wider definition of moral virtue, the identity-in-difference between ethics and the subordinate practical inquiries is retained.

To spell out both steps, consider the work of two dentists, Brace and Bridges. Brace deftly removes all the decay in Smith's molar but fills the cavity too shallowly on one side. Bridges, on the other hand, unnecessarily extracts a few of Jones's most crucial teeth, leaving the patient with a misaligned jaw. Though the problem is alleviated somewhat by expensive bridgework, the overall condition of Jones's mouth is in the end much worse than the relatively healthy condition in which it was found by Bridges on Jones's first visit. Though both dentists act with good will, the difference in their actions is evident. True, Brace errs somewhat on the side of deficiency in filling Smith's molar. A better filling would have come closer to the mean between too much and too little amalgam. All the same, his natural end as a dentist is realized. He has repaired Smith's molar.

In the case of Bridges, though, the verdict is very different. For whatever reason, Bridges has turned out to be a bad dentist. The reason is not that Bridges could have done a better job, perhaps even hitting the mean exactly. It is that Bridges has not done his job at all. In ruining instead of repairing Jones's mouth, Bridges simply fails by his actions to reach his natural end as dentist.

However, note how this contrast in the practical science of dentistry is reflected, with a difference, in the practical science of ethics. Suppose that after having repaired Smith's molar, Brace attends a meeting of the American Dental Association. There, a debate rages on the controversial subject of the fluoridation of reservoirs. Brace is convinced that the overall health risks of treating reservoirs with fluoride outweigh the benefits gained in the reduction of truth decay. Yet, when he is publicly and directly asked what his opinion is on the issue, he evades the question for fear of making enemies. Meantime, Bridges, who has entered local politics, devises a clever scheme to have his opponent Haynes murdered before the November election. On the fatal day, Bridges successfully executes his bloodthirsty plan and the murder is made to look like an accident.

Here, the parallelism between the actions of Brace and Bridges as dentists and their actions as persons can hardly be missed. Once again Brace errs on the side of deficiency. In refusing out of fear to stand up for what he believes, Brace chooses cowardice over courage in the face of public questioning. But from this one shortcoming on a single day it cannot be inferred that Brace is a bad human being, any more than it can be inferred from his failure to hit the mean in filling Smith's molar that Brace is a bad dentist. By these deficient actions, Brace's natural ends as dentist and as person, respectively, are not eliminated. But once again the case is different with Bridges. Bridges is evidently a bad person in addition to being a bad dentist. Unlike Brace's cowardice, Bridges' cold-blooded plan to murder Haynes is not wrong because it falls short of a mean. Nor is it wrong for the opposite reason of being excessive of a mean. It is wrong in principle. And just for that reason it is an act that negates his natural end as person just as his previous work on Jones' mouth blocked his natural end as dentist.

This example brings out how the foregoing dilemma is escaped. Recall that the dilemma is that defining moral virtue as a mean fails to accommodate intrinsically vicious acts while defining it as the conformity to a specific moral rule severs the tie between ethics and the other practical sciences as regards acting for the golden mean. The example shows how the dilemma is skirted by denying the consequent of its second horn. By excluding being a mean from the definition of moral virtue to cover intrinsic vice, the tie between ethics and the other practical inquiries is not broken. On the contrary, this necessary tie and order between ethics and its family members is retained. For unsatisfactory action in the crafts is not confined to excessive and deficient action; it also includes intrinsically inept action such as the dental work of Bridges. And this action perfectly parallels intrinsically vicious acts in ethics. The former subverts and contradicts the end of a person as craftsperson and the latter subverts and contradicts the end of a person as person. Bridges is not only a person whose activity fails to be the proper activity of, and hence the end and good of, a dentist; he is also a person whose activity fails to be the proper activity of, and hence the end and good of, a human being.

To cover acts that are intrinsically vicious such as murder, rape, assault, theft, perjury, etc. being a mean between extremes was excluded from the definition of moral virtue. As there are acts that are themselves vicious and not vicious just by the degree of their excess or deficiency, so there are acts that are themselves virtuous. These are acts that, like their counterparts on the side of vice, have nothing to do with falling short of or overshooting a mean. They are not right because they strike a mean. For the matter of degree is irrelevant to their moral quality just as it is in the case of acts that are intrinsically vicious. Telling the truth, keeping a promise, treating others justly, or attending to the welfare of one's children are examples of acts that are good in themselves. Exceptions to discharging one of these duties do of course occur in the case of moral conflicts. Sometimes I cannot both tell the truth and keep a promise. And other such conflicts are not uncommon. But all this implies is that intrinsically right acts that are also duties are not absolutely binding in the concrete even though they are absolutely binding in the abstract. It does not imply that they are mere guidelines or rules of thumb that are justified by the good effects that have followed their past observance. Otherwise no account is given of the difference in obligatoriness between rules that describe these intrinsically good acts, like "One ought to treat others justly," and rules like "One ought to exercise regularly."

Be that as it may, to cover these intrinsically virtuous acts, being a mean between excess and defect must be excluded from the notion of a right or virtuous act. And it was shown how this retains the hierarchical identity-in-difference between ethics and its family members in the practical disciplines. Yet, this solution invites a new problem. For widening the definition of moral virtue to accommodate intrinsic virtue implies that acting according to reason is not confined to acting prudently. It implies that it is not confined to avoiding the extremes of excess and defect in all we do. So in defining moral virtue as acting according to reason, that definition must be wide enough to catch both prudent actions and actions that are intrinsically good and not good because they strike a mean between excess and defect. Otherwise the proposed solution to the foregoing dilemma fails. But then the dilemma takes hold after all and either intrinsic virtue and vice go unaccounted for or the tie between ethics and the other practical inquiries is cut. So the question is, in what does this broader sense of "acting according to reason" consist?

A FINAL SOLUTION: NATURAL LAW ETHICS

The answer is that it consists in our actions conforming to the natural law. This answer solves the dilemma which was previously presented. Recall that that dilemma was that of either cutting the tie between ethics and the other practical sciences or failing to account for intrinsically wrong acts. Defining right acts as a mean between extremes escapes the first horn but not the second. Defining right acts as those that conform to a moral rule or as those that one does for the sake of conforming to a moral rule escapes the second horn of the dilemma but not the first. However, defining right acts as those that conform to the natural law or that accord with our nature as rational beings escapes both horns of the dilemma. For such a definition is broad enough to catch both prudent actions i.e. those that are a rational mean between irrational extremes and intrinsically virtuous actions such as telling the truth and keeping promises.

The ethics of natural law, then, offers a definition of acting virtuously that applies to both prudentially and intrinsically right acts. Utilitarians define acting rightly in terms alone of the effects of an act. And that fails to cover intrinsically right acts. And deontologists define acting virtuously in terms alone of an act's exemplifying an a priori moral rule. And that is too narrow in the other direction. It covers intrinsically right acts at the cost of excluding acts that are virtuous because they strike a mean relatively to us. But under the natural law moralist's definition of acting virtuously, the narrowness on both sides is corrected. Under this view, acts that shun both excess and defect and strike a mean are acts that accord with reason. For it is irrational to act either excessively or deficiently. But just because they accord with reason, such acts conform to and are implied by the natural law. For the natural law is based on our nature as rational beings. But acts might also be said to accord with reason when their universalizations, of which they are instances, are implied by the law of human nature. But it is a different sense of "reason" that is concerned in each case. In the former, a person acts just as a person and his/her act accords with reason in the sense of prudence. In the latter, a person acts just as a person but his/her act accords with reason in the sense of conforming to a law. Thus, acting virtuously is in all cases acting in accord with reason either in the sense of prudence or in the sense of law.

The latter sense of "acting in accord with reason" is brought out by considering the definition of intrinsically vicious acts. It may be said to be intrinsically vicious for a person s to do x if and only if, in doing x, s subverts his/her own natural end as a person. Thus, Kant is right that there is something self-defeating about intrinsically vicious acts. But this feature of intrinsically vicious acts is not spelled out the way it is in Kant. It does not consist in the fact that the maxims of such actions cannot be universalized without self-contradiction. Though that is true, it is the effect and sign of another self-defeating dimension of these acts. And that is quite literally the defeat of self. For when and to the extent that persons perform acts that are themselves vicious, they strike at their own human nature. This they do by contradicting their own natural end or good as human beings.

This is explained by showing first how what Kant says is true and then by showing why it is true. As for the first point, following the spirit if not the letter of Kant's view, it might be said that it is intrinsically vicious for a person s to do x if and only if x is done by s for the sake of satisfying selfish interest as opposed to duty or conscience and x is such that its maxim cannot be universalized without dissatisfying s's selfish interest. Thus, the maxim behind s's telling a lie is that he, s, can tell a lie whenever it suits his selfish interest, irrespective of conscience. But if this maxim is universalized to form a law to the effect that anyone at all can tell a lie whenever it suits their selfish interest irrespective of conscience, then the irony is that s's very own selfish interest is thwarted. For it is to s's selfish interest that s is told the truth by others. So, since the maxim of s's action cannot be consistently universalized by s, it follows that s's lie is intrinsically vicious.

It is not just accidental that things turn out this way in the case of lying since things turn out the same way in the case of other acts which we think are wrong in themselves. Take theft, murder, rape, assault, treating others unjustly, treating others uncharitably or breaking promises. In all these cases, persons act for the sake of selfish interest and not for the sake of duty. And yet, the acts are such that their maxims cannot be universalized without dissatisfying the selfish interest of the actor. It is to the selfish interest of thieves, murderers, rapists, assaulters, unjust persons, uncharitable persons or promise-breakers that they not be treated the way they treat others. So even on the level of selfish interest, there is an incongruity about these acts. When their maxims are subjected to the universalization of reason, the very source from which they spring, selfish interest, is threatened and so comes in conflict with itself. And so it can be said that an act t is intrinsically vicious if and only if i) t is done by a person s for the sake of satisfying s's selfish interest and ii) t is such that its maxim cannot be universalized without dissatisfying s's selfish interest.

But as was said, this inconsistency is but the sign of a deeper incongruity. This comes out as soon as it is asked why, when universalized, the maxims of these acts are self-defeating. And the answer is that such universalization flouts human nature or the law of nature for human beings. So under the Thomistic ethics, there is something which grounds and which is behind Kant's idea of the inability of wrong acts to be consistently universalized. And that is that that same inability is due to the act's flouting human nature or the law of nature for human beings.

NATURAL LAW AS GROUNDING UNIVERSALIZATION

To spell this out, recall Kant's device of universalization. In particular, consider the aforementioned universalized maxims. It may now be said that the reason behind the self-defeating aspect of these universalized maxims is that their adoption is destructive of the natural law for human beings i.e. destructive of living and acting as a human being. Thus, suppose that everyone acted on the universalizations that it is permitted to murder, steal, lie, cheat, treat others unjustly, etc., whenever it suits our selfish interests. Then, while one could live and act in the world as some kind of subhuman monster, one could not live and act in the world as a human being. Following what might be said to be the law or pattern of action for human nature would be impossible. In our life and actions we would thus be at war with ourselves. So far from being implied by the pattern of activity for human beings, actions exemplifying these universalizations would contradict that pattern. And just to that extent would those same actions fail to accord with reason — reason in the sense of law and in this case, natural law.

Take, for example, the maxim that it is allowed that I tell a lie whenever it suits my own selfish interest. The universalization of this maxim is that anyone can tell a lie whenever it suits his or her own selfish interests. But this universalization is both directed to all human beings and yet removes the trust that all human beings require to live and act as rational social animals. It therefore interferes with the pattern of activity or natural law of human beings. And just to that extent is it self-defeating in the sense of being destructive of human selves. So, since it is a universalization that conflicts with the requirements of human beings just as human beings, it follows that both it and all its concrete instances fail to accord with reason. Or take the maxim that I am allowed to ignore the poor and homeless when I am in a position to help. The universalization of this maxim is that all persons may ignore the poor and homeless when they are in a position to help the poor. This universalization is directed to human beings just as human beings and yet it recommends that what is needed to be a human being be denied to human beings, or at least to some human beings. The universalization is inconsistent in this way because it denies to human beings what human beings need to live and act as human beings. It therefore interferes with the pattern of action or natural law of human beings. So a deeper ontological (and literal) self-destructiveness lies behind the logical self-inconsistency of the universalization. If followed, the universalization would block the pattern of action or natural law of human beings. And by doing this it would once again be self-destructive in the sense of being destructive of human selves. Further, take the maxim that it is always permissible for me to treat others unjustly. The universalization of this is that anyone can treat others unjustly. But if it is followed, then this rule once again undermines the trust that is implied by the rational, social interactions of human beings. Since the universalization interferes with the law or pattern of action for human beings, it is inconsistent with that law or pattern. It would therefore be destructive of human selves because it is destructive of the natural law of human beings.

If, then, intrinsically vicious acts are wrong because they fail to accord with reason in the sense of law, we are in a better position to define intrinsically virtuous acts. Recall that these are acts that are not virtuous because they hit a mean between excess and defect but because they accord with reason in another sense. Having seen how their counterparts on the side of vice fail to accord with reason, we can now say that intrinsically virtuous acts accord with reason in this sense: so far from it being the case that their universalizations contradict the natural law of human beings, their universalizations are implied by that law or pattern.

Identifying these universalizations with the traditional rules of morality, one can then say that moral rules are hypothetical imperatives. For being implied by the law or pattern of action of human beings, they are conditioned by that same law. Moral rules are hypothetical imperatives that are conditioned by that very same law of nature for human beings. They tell us what actions must be avoided, other things being equal, if we are to conform to the law of our own nature. So far, then, from being categorical imperatives i.e. commands existing for their own sakes in regal independence, the laws of morality hang on something else. They tell us what types of action must be shunned if our lives are to conform to the law of our own nature.

But while they are hypothetical imperatives, the laws of morality are not hypothetical imperatives in the usual sense of that term. They are not conditioned by some practical or utilitarian end but by a non-pragmatic end, namely, the conformity of a thing's activity to the law of its nature. For under this theory of natural law ethics, I do not treat others justly or tell the truth or keep a promise either for the sake of my own pleasure, power, fame, wealth or health, etc., or for the sake of the pleasure, power, fame, wealth or health of the state. Otherwise moral laws are justified by the pragmatic advantages that come from following them. The moral is reduced to the expedient. And in that case, the necessity of moral laws is denied. For then moral laws begin to be obligatory when previously they were not and they can cease to be obligatory. But this is excluded by the rejection of the possibility that we may some day no longer be obliged to treat others justly and honestly. Therefore, moral rules are non-pragmatic hypothetical imperatives. Thus, since all pragmatic hypothetical imperatives are *a posteriori* then all *a priori* hypothetical imperatives, the laws of morality included, are non-pragmatic.

The reason moral laws do not either begin to be obligatory when previously they were not or cease to be obligatory (i.e. the reason they are necessary) is that they are predicated on the law of nature for human beings. Since they hold for human beings as long as and to the extent that they are human beings, therefore, moral laws neither begin to be nor can they cease to be binding on human beings. This and only this is meant here by saying moral laws are *a priori* necessary. They are not *a priori* in the sense that they are known by us since birth nor are they *a priori* in the sense that there can never be a situation in which they fail to oblige. No one but Locke's real or imagined opponent on the issue of innate ideas in his *Essay Concerning Human Understanding* believes the first, and the fact of conflict of duties falsifies the second. Rather, they are *a priori* in the sense that, unlike laws of the community or state, the laws of morality are non-pragmatic hypothetical imperatives. What is meant by this is that they are not adopted because they have been found by experience to work out. For as was said, if they wore this badge of authenticity they could be rescinded by us whenever they no longer proved to be useful. But the truth of the matter is that they cannot possibly be rescinded by us. They are in this way independent of practical experience and hence to that extent *a priori*. True, any moral law is practical in the sense of being a guide for our actions. But from this it does not follow nor is it the case that moral laws are practical in the sense of being pragmatic hypothetical imperatives, i.e. imperatives that are justified by some useful prize or reward that follows the observance of them. Moral rules are *a priori* in the sense that they are neither confirmed nor confuted by appeal to sense experience. Rather, such laws are automatically seen to be true by anyone who understands what it means to be a human being, by anyone who understands what the law of nature is for human beings. And since we are human beings, this law is better known by most of us than is the law of any other nature.

Moreover, under this ethics of natural law, acts are not right in themselves because they benefit humankind but they benefit humankind because they are right in themselves. For an act is right if and only if it accords with the law of nature of the actor and the good of the species is the effect of that conformity. That is one reason it is called a natural law ethics. When a tomato plant follows the law of its nature, it produces seeds and this is beneficial to the tomato species. When a human being follows the law of his/her nature he/she produces rational actions and these are beneficial to the human species. Thus, just to the extent that society always benefits from right acts, the natural law ethics has a built-in social dimension. That, among other things, is what separates it from radically egoistic ethical theories like that of Epicurus. If our actions have the effect of harming human society it follows that they cannot be intrinsically right actions. For as was said, in natural law ethics one consequence of intrinsically right acts is that they are acts that tend to benefit humankind.

But though it cannot live without this social dimension, natural law ethics nonetheless compatibly denies the claim of utilitarianism that acts are right because they promote the good of society. For this is to confuse a property of right acts with the definition of a right act. True, tending to promote the common good is a property of all right acts *qua* right. That is the strength of utilitarianism and explains why utilitarianism is seen as corrective of egoism. But like many other valuable antitheses it overshoots the mark, overcompensating for the deficiency of the thesis. For no sooner is the promotion of the common good made the definition of a right act than no account is possible of the evident necessity of moral laws. For under utilitarianism moral laws are justified on the basis of practical experience. And so they are pragmatic hypothetical imperatives. But then moral laws are *a posteriori* in which case it must be countenanced (absurdly) that our obligation to treat others justly and honestly might some day be rescinded.

SUMMARY AND DEFINITIONS

Natural law ethics agrees with rule-deontologism in holding that any act is *prima facie* right if it exemplifies a necessary moral law. But siding with a deontologist like Ross rather than with one like Kant, it holds that moral laws describe what our duty is *prima facie*, not what our duty is in a concrete moral situation. This allows for the settlement of conflicts of duties. If under a set of circumstances c I am torn between telling the truth and keeping a promise when I cannot do both, it cannot be said, under both Ross's and the natural law views, that I am being absolutely commanded to do something that it is impossible for me to do if moral rules describe what our duties are *prima facie* and not absolutely. This can only be said under the ethics if Kant. Such conflicts are resolved by calculating what the effects are of following each rule under c and then acting on the rule conformity to which brings the least harmful results for all concerned. And it is important to see that the action that satisfies this latter criterion is not obligatory just because it better promotes the common good than does the act that follows the other rule. Rather is it obligatory because it better promotes the common good than does the action that follows the other rule and is also an instance of a moral rule. Thus, in all conflicts of duties, the act that conforms to the rule that, if followed in the situation in question, promotes the greater good of all concerned is right and obligatory in the concrete, while the act that conforms to the other rule is obligatory in the abstract or *prima facie* but not obligatory in the concrete or actually.

But while it agrees with rule deontologism in judging actions to be *prima facie* right in themselves when they conform to *a priori* moral laws (in the sense of *a priori* that has been specified), the natural law ethics departs from the rule ethics on the status of these laws. They are not construed as unconditioned or categorical imperatives but as imperatives that follow upon the rational nature of human beings. For while any act t is intrinsically right, at least *prima facie*, if t conforms to a moral law m, m is a moral law in the first place only if it describes a way of acting to which human beings are naturally inclined. And they are inclined by their natures to rational actions since they are rational animals. Ultimately, therefore, any action t is right if and only if t conforms to the human nature of the actor.

Acts that fall under a moral law are right because they are obligatory. For all *prima facie* obligatory acts are *prima facie* right acts. But it does not follow that all right acts are obligatory. This is shown in the case of heroic acts. It would not be wrong for a weak swimmer to refrain from trying to help a person who is in danger of drowning. But if the attempt is made, the act is commendable and right. From this it follows that though acts that fall under a moral law are right, not all right acts fall under a moral law. Right acts, therefore, cannot be defined as those acts that conform to a moral law. In fact, conformity to a moral law is neither a necessary nor a sufficient condition of the rightness of any concrete act. Instead, the concept of moral rightness is no different from the relational concept of the fitting or the appropriate, where the measure of the fittingness or appropriateness is human nature.

From this the following definitions emerge under the ethics of natural law:

D1. x is the good of a person s as person = df x is the natural end of s.

D2. action *t* is implied by the natural end of a person s as person = df either *t* conforms to a moral rule or *t* is a mean relative to s's acting as a person.

D3. action *t* is morally right = df either *t* is implied by the natural end of a person s or *t* is a supererogatory act.

D4. action *t* is intrinsically right = df *t* conforms to a moral rule.

D5. a person s is *prima facie* obliged to perform action *t* = df *t* is implied by the natural end of s.

D6. a person s is actually obliged to perform action *t* = df (i) s is *prima facie* obliged to perform *t* and (ii) either a) there is not another act *n* such that s is also *prima facie* obliged to do *n* or else b) when s cannot perform both *t* and *n*, s's performing *t* has more of an excess of good over bad consequences for those concerned than does s's performing *n*.

Under these definitions, an act's being obligatory implies that it is either intrinsically or prudentially virtuous and *vice versa*. Second, an act's being obligatory implies that it is right but not *vice versa*. Third, an act's being right both implies and is implied by its being either intrinsically virtuous, prudentially virtuous or morally heroic or supererogatory. Fourth, under these same definitions, since an act's being prudentially virtuous or a mean of action implies that it is *prima facie* obligatory and an act's being supererogatory does not imply this, it follows that prudentially virtuous acts and supererogatory or morally heroic acts are different kinds of right acts.

The foregoing definitions also show that in natural law ethics rightness is defined in terms of goodness. For goodness has the nature of an end, and rightness is defined in terms of the human natural end. They also show that obligatoriness is defined in terms of rightness when the latter has the sense of what is implied by the human natural end. And since the natural end of a thing is its good, it follows that obligatoriness is defined in terms of good. The definitions thus reflect the view of Aquinas that in ethics the idea of natural end or goodness is fundamental. They also echo his belief that falling under a moral rule is neither a necessary nor a sufficient condition of an act's being right in the concrete. It is not a necessary condition because supererogatory acts are right without being obliged. And it is not a sufficient condition because, in the case of a conflict of rules, an act might conform to a moral rule and yet not be actually or in the concrete the right thing to do, even though it is *prima facie* right. What is both a necessary and sufficient condition of an act's being right, as was said, is that it actually conforms to the natural end of human beings.

OBJECTIONS AND REPLIES

It might be objected that natural law ethics diminishes the importance of moral rules in ethics. But this objection comes only from pure deontologists like Kant. And these deontologists so elevate moral rules as to make them prodigious. This is shown by the contradiction in which all pure deontologists are implicated. For when moral rules are elevated to the point of being absolutized, then, in cases of conflicting duties, persons are sometimes absolutely commanded to do what they cannot possibly do. You do not devalue moral rules when you refuse to absolutize them. You save them from irresolvable contradiction in their application. It is not the natural law moralist but the utilitarian who diminishes moral principles. This he does by reducing moral principles to pragmatic hypothetical imperatives, thereby ruining their *prima facie* necessity.

Second, it might be objected that natural law ethics understates the role that consequences play in determining what acts are right. And to obviate this criticism, so the objection would run, the natural law moralist can only define a right act as one that promotes the best possible consequences. However, it was shown that this utilitarian definition implies that standard moral principles have a purely pragmatic function; they revert to being expedient as opposed to being truly ethical hypothetical imperatives. As such, they begin to be binding only when we human beings judged that it is expedient to observe them and they cease to be imperatives if they are judged by us to be useless. But with Kant, one can only protest that this radically empiricist account of moral rules undermines the necessity of moral rules, even though that necessity is a *prima facie* and not an absolute necessity. We accept the possibility of finding white crows in Cracow, but neither in Cracow nor in Caracas do we accept the possibility that it might some day be right to manipulate persons as if they were mere objects or means to our selfish ends.

The reply to a third objection brings out more clearly the concept of right action in natural law ethics. This third objection is that in this ethics the definition of rightness is too broad. If an act that strikes a mean relatively to us is right, it follows that I act rightly when, erring neither on the side of excess or defect in any way, I successfully teach logic. Yet, this is evidently neither right nor wrong but morally neutral. Hence, the definition of a right act in D3 above is too broad.

But this objection feeds on a misreading of the definition. For under D3. a right act is not simply any act at all that is a mean relatively to us, but an act that is a mean relatively to us acting just as persons. It must be the sort of act that is or can be performed by a human being *qua* human being. This reflects the universality of ethics as over against the other practical inquiries to which reference was previously made. But successfully getting across the principles of logic to undergraduates is far from being the act of a human being just as human. It is something that a person does or can do only in some specialized capacity, namely, as gifted or experienced teacher. But then it is not counted as being a right act in natural law ethics. And if it is not, then no one successfully objects that, because it does count such an act as being morally right, the definition of a right act in D3. is too broad.

A fourth objection is that natural law ethics illicitly concludes an "ought" from an "is," a statement of obligation from a statement of fact. For just because human nature is what it is, how does it follow that our actions ought to conform to it? Or put negatively, just because human nature is what it is, how does it follow that our actions ought not to flout it? Statements of obligation, like statements of value, are not implied by statements of fact.

To answer, it is not human nature in a purely descriptive, factual sense that according to natural law ethics is the ground of obligation. As the name "natural law" suggests, it is the law of human nature that is the ground of obligation. It is not so much because human nature is what it is that our actions ought to conform to it; rather, it is because the law of human nature is what it is that our actions ought to conform to it. And that makes all the difference. For 'law' here refers not to descriptive, factual law (i.e. 'law' in the sense of 'statistical uniformity') but to teleological law. Since it is the law of human nature from which obligation is deduced and since this law is to begin with no matter of fact, then the objection that natural law ethics deduces statements of obligation from statements of fact misses the mark.

But to say that this teleological law is not fact is not to say what it is. So to round out their reply and make it credible, defenders of natural law ethics must specify what is meant by the law of nature of a thing. This is done by identifying the law of nature of a thing with those features or activities of a thing that *would* issue from a thing's nature, other things being equal. Recurring to the tomato plant, we say that the activities involved in the development of fruit and seeds are just those activities that would issue from the plant, other things being equal. The word 'would' here is important. It shows that the law referred to in 'law of a thing's nature' falls under the category of *would-be* as opposed to the category of fact.[18] It also shows the point of view from which a thing's nature is considered when we speak of the law of its nature. The point of view is that of final causality. And so the law of a thing's nature, its *would-be*, and its final cause all come to the same thing. But if so, then in holding that it is because the law of human nature is what it is that we humans ought to act in conformity to it, natural law ethics cannot be charged with deducing a statement of obligation from a statement of fact. For what the law of human nature is in the first place is law and not fact. Since the law of a thing's nature is a *would-be* and not an *is* in the sense of a brute fact to begin with, then the obligation that is deduced therefrom is not deduced from the purely factual.

True, in espousing the principle that those activities that would issue from a thing are activities that ought to issue from the thing, natural law ethics does deduce an ought-statement from a would-statement. And the objection might be that this is no more valid than inferring an ought-statement from an is-statement. But such an objection misses the point. For in natural law ethics, to use a would-statement in the sense of expressing the law of nature or *would-be* of a thing is just another way of saying what the thing naturally ought to do. I say of my tomato plant that it ought to be flowering at a certain stage and that it ought to be bearing fruit at another stage. And it is evident that the "ought" here refers to the law of its nature. But the law of its nature is exactly what is referred to when it is said of activities in the plant that they are activities that would issue from the plant. Therefore, since their sense of 'ought' in this connection expresses the law of a thing's nature, and since in their view how a thing would act also refers to the law of its nature, defenders of natural law ethics do not illicitly deduce activities that ought to issue from a thing from activities that would issue from a thing.

A fifth and final objection cuts even deeper than the fourth. It is simply that there is no such thing as the law of nature or final cause of a thing. And in that case the very idea of an ethics of natural law is a *hirngespinst*. The centrality of this objection is seen by reviewing the pattern of the argument. A thing's good is identified with the law of its nature and the latter is what directs the activities of a thing to its end. But since this is the definition of final cause, it follows that a thing's good is identified with its final cause.

But ever since Galileo final causality has been eliminated. Early modern science showed that Aristotle's explanations by final cause were dispensable. For the same phenomena could be explained by the new mathematical physics. And one advantage of this new type of explanation was that it was susceptible, as the presence of a final cause was not, of empirical verification. Another was that because under this new explanation natural events were for the first time seen as instances of necessary, mathematically precise laws, explanation took on a rationality it could never even hope to have achieved under teleological explanation. Lacking the rationality and verifiability of the new physics, therefore, explanation by final cause came to be looked on and is still regarded by many as being metaphysical explanation. Here, 'metaphysical' almost has the same sense as 'theological.' Metaphysical explanation is just religious explanation incarnated. For under both explanations the *explanans* is a hidden, occult entity or power, exercising a controlling influence over natural events. It is just that in explaining a natural event by final cause instead of by the will of God you move the unsensed power from heaven to earth. For as was said, a final cause is the innermost principle of a thing defining the law of its nature.

But the assumption behind this objection is that only those entities that are needed and verified by science are real. But imagine the situation reversed and a moralist announces that only those entities that are needed by ethics are real. Such entities might be, for example, non-natural properties, the true Self, or The Practical Will. Everyone would charge the moralist with moralism, i.e. with identifying the real with the ethical. The complaint would be that, carried away with his enthusiasm for ethics, the moralist inflates ethics out of all proportion, making it a prodigy. How, then, do those who identify the real with what is needed and verified by science escape scientism, i.e. the identification of the real with the scientific? And if they do not, how is their scientism less narrow and one-sided than moralism? Not just that but, more positively, it was shown in Chapter Three that final causes appeared to be necessary in order to account for immanent changes in living things. So whereas final causes might not be required for some natural sciences, they nonetheless seem to be required for biology, at least to the extent that biology concerns the explanation of immanent changes in living things.

Moreover, though teleology might be unnecessary for most sciences, it does seem to be necessary for ethics. For it is required by the fact of right action. It is required by the fact that some human actions are right in the only sense in which it has here been argued it makes sense to say they are right, namely, that they are actions that conform to the *telos* or law of nature for human beings.

NOTES

1. St. Thomas Aquinas, *Summa theologica* in A. Pegis, trans. *Intoduction to St. Thomas Aquinas* (New York: The Modern Library, 1948) I-II, q. 94, a. 2, 635–638.
2. Ibid., *Summa theologica,* trans. A. Pegis, I, q. 5, a. 4, 39–41.
3. See Aristotle, *Nicomachean Ethics*, trans. Terence Irwin (Indianapolis: Hackett publishing Co., 1985), Book I, 1097a, 15–1097b, 7; 13-14.
4. See Aristotle, *Nicomachean Ethics*, trans. Terence Irwin, Book I, 1098a, 3–19; 16–17.
5. St. Thomas Aquinas, *Summa contra gentiles,* Book III, Ch. XXV and XXXVIII.
6. Aquinas states that no agent acts except for an end. See Aquinas, *Summa theologica* trans. A. Pegis, I, q. 5, a. 2, reply obj. 1, 37. See also, *Summa theologica* I, q. 44, a. 4, 239–241.
7. Aquinas holds that every agent acts for an end or else one thing would not follow more than anything else from an agent's action. See *Summa theologica*, trans. A. Pegis, I, q. 44, a. 4, 239–241.
8. See Chapter III, 60–67.
9. This is a broader sense of the term 'natural law' than that which Aquinas specifies in his *Summa theologica*. There, Aquinas defines natural law as the rational creature's participation of the eternal law. See *Summa theologica*, trans. A. Pegis, I–II q. 91, a. 2, 617–619.
10. See the argument for this in Chapter Three, 76–80.
11. Aquinas holds that the proper objects of the human intellect are forms as existing in corporeal matter but not as existing in this or that individual matter. See Aquinas, *Summa theologica* trans. A. Pegis, I, q. 85, a. 1, 400–407.
12. See chapter III, 60–72.
13. St. Thomas Aquinas, *Summa theologica* trans. A. Pegis, I, q. 6, a. 4, 50–52.
14. St. Thomas Aquinas, *Commentary on the Trinity of Boethius*, q. 5,a. 1, in *An Introduction to the Metaphysics of St. Thomas Aquinas*, trans. James F. Anderson (Chicago: Henry Regnery Co., 1953), Chapter One, 3–15.
15. St. Thomas Aquinas, *Summa theologica* trans. A. Pegis, I–II, q. 94, a. 2, 635–638.

16. See Aristotle, *Nicomachean Ethics* trans. Terence Irwin, Book II, 1103b, l. 26–28, 35.

17. Aquinas states that ends or final causes are not operative in mathematics since mathematical objects like numbers are abstracted from matter and change. See Aquinas, *Summa theologica* trans. A. Pegis, I, q. 5 a. 3, reply obj. 4, 41.

18. It is C.S. Peirce who is chiefly responsible for calling attention to the difference between the categories of law (would-be) and fact. Peirce usually calls them the categories of third and second, respectively. Though it goes too far to say that 'law' in 'law of a thing's nature' has the very same sense in natural law ethics as the category of law has in Peirce, it is interesting to note the following: Peirce holds that the category of law includes the idea of thought or meaning and Peirce's pragmaticism implies that all thought or meaning is purposeful. So in Peirce law is inextricably linked to purpose or teleology. Be that as it may, Peirce and the natural law moralist agree in distinguishing the lawful from the factual. See Hartshorne and Weiss, editors, *Collected Papers of C.S. Peirce*, (Cambridge: Harvard University Press, 1931–35), 1.343, 345–7.

Chapter Seven

Universals

Chapter One outlined the scholastic distinction between essence and existence. Because 'essence' is often used synonymously with 'universal,' and because a thing's act of existence is taken to be the instantiation of some essence, the essence-existence distinction prompts the question of the status of universals and their relation to particulars. This defines the issue of universals in philosophy. In any case, the view of Aquinas and others that essences or universals have ontological status apart from minds is known as realism. This is realism as opposed to both nominalism, which denies essences or universals outright, and conceptualism, which countenances them as mind-dependent only. Universals, say conceptualists, are only in minds as so many abstract ideas.

In its extreme form, realism holds that universals are things in their own right which are exemplified by things of a fundamentally different sort, namely particulars. The classic statement and defense of this extreme realism is found in Plato. Thus, in "Socrates is human" Socrates exemplifies the universal or property of being human where 'Socrates' and 'human' refer to two very different kinds of thing which enter into the relation of exemplification. Socrates, it is said, exemplifies the universal human. Among objections to this extreme realism is that it in one way or another implies an infinite regress and so is untenable. However, even if this is true, it scarcely follows that either nominalism or conceptualism is true. For a less extreme form of realism is moderate or scholastic realism. And it might just be the case that the latter escapes these alleged regresses. And in what follows I argue (A) not only that scholastic realism escapes these regress problems but that, in addition, (B) only moderate realism of the scholastic type allows for the possibility of predication. But first the following six definitions are in order:

s is an extreme realist = df s holds that universals exist independently of space-time and hence independently of matter and mind.

s is a moderate realist = df (i) s denies that universals exist independently of space-time and (ii) s affirms that universals exist only in and through particulars.

s is an Aristotelian realist = df (i) s is a moderate realist and (ii) s denies that universals exist in any transcendent particular such as a transcendent mind.

s is a scholastic realist = df (i) s is a moderate realist and (ii) s holds that universals exist immanently in and through spatial-temporal particulars and transcendently in God's mind.

s is a conceptualist = df (i) s denies that universals exist extra-mentally either immanently in and through particulars or transcendently, and (ii) s affirms that universals exist in minds.

s is a nominalist = df s denies that universals have ontological status of any kind, i.e. either immanently in and through particulars (be they bodies or minds) or transcendently.

Taking points (A) and (B) in order, let us begin with the extreme realism or platonism of Bertrand Russell. In his early philosophy, Russell held 1) that there are such things as simple or atomic facts which exist independently of being known and 2) that every such fact is a complex of at least one particular and a universal. Examples of these are i) the fact that *a* is white, ii) the fact that *a* is to the left of *b*, and iii) the fact that *a* is between *b* and *c*. Taken respectively, 1) and 2) show that at this stage Russell is both a realist as opposed to an idealist and a realist as distinct from a nominalist. These two realisms might be called metaphysical and platonic realism, respectively.[1] As for 1), he takes it as a datum that the fact that Edinburgh is north of London (to use his example) exists whether anyone knows it or not. That being the case, the universal 'north of' must also exist apart from minds. For, says Russell, nothing that contains what is mental can be non-mental. So if the fact in question is evidently non-mental then so too is the universal 'north of' which figures in it. Thus, going by the rule that nothing non-mental contains something mental, Russell infers platonic realism from metaphysical realism.[2]

This sparks the issue of universals. If a universal is one as opposed to the many particulars which instance it, how is it possible that 'north of,' which figures in the fact that Edinburgh is north of London, also figures in the facts that Boston is north of New York, that Chicago is north of St. Louis, and so on? If universals are by definition one, then if the fact that Edinburgh is north of London includes the universal 'north of,' how can 'north of' also enter into other facts?

It was due to their Aristotelianism that this problem of universals disturbed medieval scholastics. If Plato's Forms are not separate and independent but rather inherent in and dependent on their exemplifications, then the realism-nominalism controversy looms large. Being universal, forms are one. So if Aristotelians say that the form humanity is present in Socrates, then they must justify their view that it is also present in Plato. This they can never do, say nominalists. Since what is one cannot be many, to instantiate Plato's Forms is to eliminate them. True, in 'Socrates is human' and 'Plato is human' the predicate 'human' might be construed as signifying a universal. But since universals cannot be many, that only shows that language is misleading. False ontologies can come from assuming a one-to-one correspondence between language and the world. Saying that Socrates and Plato are both human is just our way of expressing their similarity. And that similarity is ultimate and irreducible. To think otherwise and say that besides these two individuals, there is in each one of them some abstract thing 'humanity' which is needed to ground their similarity is unnecessary as well as impossible. Entities ought not to be needlessly admitted. Besides, multiplying a form or universal according to the diversity of individuals to which the name of that form or universal applies is impossible. Being one, no form or universal can be present in many.

Now whatever objections can be raised against platonic realism, it seems that this nominalist one is not one of them. The reason is that under the latter realism a simple fact such as 'a is white' denotes an external and not an internal relation between a and whiteness. In the view of Plato, the early Russell and more recently Gustav Bergmann, the universal whiteness is not to begin with a part or constituent of an individual like a. Instead, a universal is something separated from particulars. True, for Plato the particular thing a is a copy or reflection of whiteness whereas for Russell and Bergmann a is not even that. It is nothing but a bare x or in the words of Bergmann, a bare particular.[3] But the point is that for neither philosopher is it true to say that a really *is* white or that whiteness is present in a. Instead, a exemplifies whiteness, where 'exemplifies' denotes an external relation or tie between two things of different kinds, a particular and a universal. So, since they deny in the first instance that universals are present in particulars — holding instead that it is one and the same separated universal that is exemplified by many particulars — platonic realists escape the contradiction of saying that universals are one and yet multiplied in many. Therefore, as against this realism the foregoing nominalist objection cuts no ice. It is relevant only to the moderate realism of Aristotle and the scholastics. So using that objection against Plato's, Russell's, Bergmann's or any other platonic realist's arguments for universals misses the mark.

Nevertheless, a stock objection to platonic realism is that it implies an infinite regress. And celebrated denials of realism have turned on that claim.

Of these, Plato's "third-man" objection to the Forms in the *Parmenides* is most familiar.[4] If Socrates and Plato are human by virtue of exemplifying the Form Humanity, must we not then say that Socrates and Plato on the one hand and Humanity on the other are also human? And if so, must they not be human by virtue of exemplifying a second-order Humanity? But to continue, if Socrates, Plato, first-order Humanity and second-order Humanity are all human, must not they be human by still another, third-order Humanity, and so on without end? To generalize, if there are two things a and b that are F, whether F is the Form of Humanity or any other Form, and if the following three dicta are true, then an infinite number of Forms of F on succeeding levels is incurred.

    A If there are distinct things that are F, then there is a Form F in which they participate.
    B The Form F is itself F.
    C If something participates in the Form F, then it is not identical with F.[5]

A second type of regress-objection is Ryle's. For platonic realists, the relation of 'white' to 'a' is an instance of exemplification. But its being in that relation to exemplification is an instance of a second-level exemplification, and that, in turn, is an instance of a third-level exemplification, and so on, *ad infinitum*.[6]

To explain, under the realist's assay, a's exemplifying F and b's exemplifying F are two instances of the relational universal of exemplification, E. Thus we have,

    <<a,F>, E> and
    <<b,F>, E>

But these two instances of E are instances of a higher-level exemplification E. Thus,

    <<<a,F>,E>, E1>> and
    <<<b,F>,E>, E1>>

But now these two new instances of exemplification exemplify a still higher-order exemplification, E2, and so on to infinity. While it might not be vicious, this regress of E's is unacceptable. It follows, says Ryle, that 'a is white' "is not a relational proposition" or in other words, that the extreme realist's assay of 'a is white' as a relation between a particular and a universal is impossible.

Nor, to cap the regress at its source, can realists reply that what the ordered pairs

<<a,F>,E>, <<<a,F>,E>,E1>>, <<<<a,F>,E>,E1>,E2>>>, etc., and
<<b,F>,E>, <<<b,E>,E1>>, <<<<b,F>,E>,E1>,E2>>>, and so on

all exemplify is one and the same exemplification-relation E, and not, respectively, E, E1, E2, and so on. Thus,

<<a,F>,E>, <<<a,F>,E>,E>>, <<<<a,F>,E>,E>,E>>> etc., and
<<b,F>,E>, <<<b,F>,E>,E>>, <<<<b,F>,E>,E>,E>>> etc., and so on

This gambit only spells a category mistake. For it is the same thing E that is both part of what exemplifies and what is exemplified, appearing both on the left side and on the right side of the very same instance of exemplification.

A third type of regress-objection to platonic realism invokes Bradley's argument against any and all external relations, exemplification included.[7] If 'a is white' signifies that a and white are two things tied by the (external) relation of exemplification R, then, a and R beings things, you need a further thing, R1, to link a to R. But a and R1 being things too, you need a further thing again, R2, to join a and R1, and so on to infinity. So a cannot be tied to whiteness by the relation of exemplification. This regress is putatively vicious since it is alleged that for a to be linked to whiteness an infinite number of relations must first be posited. In this it recalls Zeno's disproof of motion. Since to move from point A to point B, says Zeno, an arrow must traverse an infinite number of points, the motion of the arrow is illusory. Be that as it may, it follows that platonic realism is wrong and no one correctly construes 'a is white' as an external relation between a particular and a universal.

To skirt the first and second regresses, platonic realists might invoke the Theory of Types. As regards the third-man puzzle, that theory would render statements of self-predication meaningless. You can say that Socrates is human or that Plato is human but under the Theory of Types it is nonsense to say that Humanity is human. That is because the theory stipulates that any predicate P on level L is meaningfully applied only to what is on level L-1. Thus premise B above, on which the third-man argument depends, is false. Alternatively, the objection thrives on ignoring the gap between subjects and predicates. "…Predicates are taken formally, and subjects materially," says Aquinas.[8] In other words, subjects signify what is in some way material or what is receptive of form. They indicate what is participatively-F and not what is just F. Therefore, you cannot meaningfully make a Form, or what is just F, a subject. True, we do say things like "Humanity is timeless." However, platonic realists can always reply that such statements are not subject-predicate statements.

One might also plausibly use The Theory of Types to stifle Ryle's regress. You can say (i) that a and b are green and (ii) that each one of them being green is an instance of Exemplification. But under the Theory of Types it is nonsense to go on and say (iii) that these two instances of Exemplification are in turn instances of Exemplification. True, the second Exemplification in (iii) is putatively on a higher level than the first, so that saying this seems to follow the requirement that any predicate P on level L is meaningfully applied only to what is on level L-1. But that will not do. For under the theory, L is not just the same kind of quality or relation as L-1 (as is here the case) but a wider quality or relation, as animal is different from and wider than human. So under the theory, if the first Exemplification in (iii) is on level L-1, then what is on level L is not a *second* Exemplification but the wider category of relation, of which the first Exemplification is a sub-set. But if so, then (iii) is meaningless. However, since (iii) is needed to instigate Ryle's regress, it follows that the latter is blocked from the very start. Saying in (iii) that these two instances of Exemplification are in turn instances of a second Exemplification flouts the Theory of Types no less than saying that Humanity is human.

That leaves Bradley's regress. Since it is not self-predication that instigates the latter, it is unavailing to invoke the Theory of Types to thwart this regress. But though it does not spring from self-predication, the Bradleian regress feeds on another assumption. As Bergmann points out, the regress takes hold only if it is assumed that exemplification is a thing like the two things it ties, say, *a* and whiteness.[9] If what links two things is itself a thing, then we are off to the races. You then need a second link to tie the first one to the things it ties, and so on down the line. However, says Bergmann, since the assumption is false, no regress accrues. So far from being a thing, exemplification is a fundamental tie. Unlike things, fundamental ties like exemplification (and, he would add, meaning) are like Aristotle's accidents as opposed to his substances. They do not exist in themselves or in their own right but always exist in and through what does exist that way.[10] And since for platonic realists what does exist in itself is a thing and things are either particulars or universals, then the exemplification-tie exists either in and through a particular or in and through a universal. Either particulars have the built-in relational property of being tied to universals or universals have the internal character of being tied to particulars. Figuratively, either one comes equipped with the glue that ties it to the other. In either case, no *tertium quid* is needed to join them. Instead, the two fit together, as Wittgenstein said of his objects, "like the links of a chain."[11] And with this the Bradleian regress dies in the starting-gate.

Yet nominalists would counter that Bergmann's move is only fodder for their mill. True, by means of it you dodge Bradley's regress by demoting exemplification from being an independent, Platonic universal to being a dependent, Aristotelian one. But in so doing you only resurrect the foregoing query that led some scholastics to nominalism. The only difference is that instead of bearing on qualitative universals like humanity, it hones in on the relational universal of exemplification. If humanity is one and in Socrates, asked some scholastics, how can it also be in Plato? Just so, assuming that *a* is white and *b* is green, if exemplification is one and is either in *a* or in white, then how can it also be in *b* or in green? This tempts some to deny that it is the same exemplification each time, just as the corresponding query about humanity tempted some schoolmen to deny that it was the same humanity that was in Socrates and Plato. Yielding to the temptation in either case putatively abandons realism for nominalism. It seems, therefore, that platonic realists are checkmated. They either succumb to Bradley's regress or become nominalists.

The way out of this for realists is to embrace scholastic realism. To see how the latter gets between nominalism and the regress, recall the query that led some medieval thinkers to nominalism. If humanity is one and present in Socrates, then how can it also be present in Plato? The answer of scholastic realists is that though humanity is surely present in Socrates, it is not necessarily one. So there is no reason why it cannot be multiplied in many which it in fact is. Any nature like humanity is in itself neither numerically one nor numerically many. It is entirely neutral as between the two.[12] Being one or many in number are properties which a nature acquires as a result of its being quantified. They are not properties that belong to any nature taken as such. Otherwise the following pseudo-syllogisms are countenanced:

Socrates and Plato are human.
Human is one.
Hence, Socrates and Plato are one.

And,

Socrates is human.
Human is many.
So Socrates is many.

By analogy, the properties of being a species or being a genus do not belong to a nature or essence taken just as such.[13] They are properties that an essence takes on only as a result of being known. Otherwise we invite the following:

Socrates is human.
Human is a species.
So Socrates is a species.[14]

In sum, if humanity is necessarily numerically one, it cannot be numerically many. But it *is* many in Socrates, Plato, Callias, etc. And if humanity is necessarily numerically many, then it cannot be numerically one. But it *is* one in Socrates. One and not many humanities are present in Socrates. It follows that humanity (and by extension every other essence) is in itself neither numerically one nor numerically many. Instead, being one or many in number are properties that are accidental to humanity, just as are the properties of being a species and being a genus.

Yet nominalists would counter that, no less than platonic realism, this more moderate realism fails to dodge the dilemma in question. The many humanities that are multiplied in Socrates, Plato, Callias, etc. are each one of them unique and unrepeatable. Socrates' humanity is not Plato's and Plato's is not Callias's. Each one of these humanities then ceases to be universal and becomes particular. Therefore, so far from sidestepping the dilemma of incurring Bradley's regress or espousing nominalism, scholastic realists meet the same fate as Bergmann. They avoid the regress only by surrendering their realism for nominalism.

However, realists of a Thomistic stripe would parry this counter-reply by distinguishing two senses of 'one.'[15] True, humanity is multiplied in Socrates, Plato, Callias, etc. Yet the paradox is that this many-ness does not exclude its also being one in these and all other persons. It all depends on what you mean by 'one.'

To spell it out, humanity's being either numerically one or many is consequent on its being quantified just as humanity's being a genus or a species is consequent on its being known. What are numerically one or many are individual humans or horses and not humanity or horseness itself taken apart from existing in individuals as spatial objects or in minds as universal concepts. There is an analogy in arithmetic. What are numerically one or many are not twoness or threeness taken as such but individual two's and three's. True, these are not in physical space like individual humans and horses but they are nonetheless in what might be called intelligible space.[16] Here the quantity is not physical but intelligible. When we put planks together to make a shed, we acknowledge that the result, i.e. the shed, is larger than any one of the planks. Similarly, when we add five ones together to make five, we say that the result, i.e. five, is larger than any one of the ones. The evident difference is that in the former "larger than" refers to physical space or physical quantity whereas in the latter "larger than" refers to mathematical space or intelligible quantity.

And yet, the numerically many and similar humanities in Socrates, Plato and Callias are nonetheless one or undivided *in definition* just as in arithmetic the ones I add up, though five in number, are one or undivided in definition. Here, oneness or unity follows on being in the sense of quiddity or objective sense. It is the unity behind definition and not a quantitative unity.[17] What is numerically divided might be in definition undivided. For whether humanity exists intentionally in minds or really in Socrates or other persons, it is in each one of these modes or conditions one and the same in objective sense. Otherwise internal division breaks out in the very definition of 'human.' And since genus and difference comprise the definition, that amounts to saying that either the genus or the difference is split. If the latter, then 'human' is defined as a rational or a non-rational animal. The *differentia* here having been lost by the divisive disjunct, "rational or non-rational," 'human' then covers brutes as well as ourselves. If the former, then 'human' is defined as a rational animal or non-animal. The proximate genus here having been compromised by the divisive disjunct, "animal or non-animal," 'human' then covers rational pure spirits as well as ourselves. In either case, since either being rational or being an animal ends up being accidental to a human being, this conceptual rift in the definition of 'human' obliterates its determinate sense.

So despite the fact that there are as many humanities as there are individual persons, they all of them have the same definition. And to the extent that this definition is one with respect to many, it is universal. And this universality or oneness in definition that belongs to the many similar humanities exists quite independently of minds. Thus, it is this simultaneous unity in sense or definition that it has alongside of its numerical many-ness that allows us to say compatibly (if paradoxically) that in Socrates, Plato, Callias, etc. humanity is many and particular even as it is one and universal. When in these individuals it is being in the sense of quantity that is concerned, humanity is many in all three. But when it is being in the sense of essence or definition that is concerned, humanity is one for all three.

Now what with these diverse senses of 'one' in place — the one supervening on being as quantity and the other on being as essence or objective sense — is it not now possible for modern realists like Russell, Moore, and Bergmann to avoid Bradley's regress without sacrificing realism for nominalism? For to do the former, all they need do is to exchange their platonic realism for a Thomistic moderate realism under which Plato's transcendent essences are instantiated. Then, since nothing is needed in the first place to link a particular to some transcendent property, Bradley's regress becomes a hoax. And to do the latter, all they need do is to espouse the distinction between being one in number and being one or undivided in definition or objective sense. They can then say that, despite being multiplied in many, essences like humanity in Socrates, Plato, Callias, etc. remain formally or in definition one in these individuals, a unity which accrues to them independently of minds. But their being one in that sense is sufficient to ward off the consequence that all there is is purely particular which, along with Ockham's Razor, comprises the centerpiece of nominalism.

NOTES

1. By 'platonic realism' here and in what follows it is meant the idea that universals are mind-independent, self-subsisting entities. This is wide enough to cover views of universals

(such as Plato's, Russell's and Bergmann's) that are otherwise different. Hence, the reason for the lower-case 'p' in 'platonic.'

2. Russell, Bertrand, *The Problems of Philosophy* (London: Oxford University Press, 1974), 98.

3. Gustav Bergmann, "Stenius on the *Tractatus*" in *Logic and Reality* (Madison: University of Wisconsin Press, 1964), 246. See also, Gustav Bergmann, "Strawson's Ontology" in *Logic and Reality*, 175, 185.

4. Plato, *Parmenides* 131c–132b; 132c–133a. in *The Dialogues of Plato* trans. B. Jowett (London: Oxford University Press, 1953), vol. II, 674–75; 676–677.

5. F. J. Pelletier and E. N. Zalta, "How to Say Goodbye to the Third Man" *Nous*, 34/2 (June 2000), 168.

6. Gilbert Ryle, "Plato's 'Parmenides'" in *Studies in Plato's Metaphysics,* ed. R. E. Allen (New York: The Humanities Press, 1965), 107.

7. F.H. Bradley, *Appearance and Reality*, (London: Oxford University Press, 1962), 22–28.

8. St. Thomas Aquinas, *Summa theologica*, in A. Pegis, trans., *Introduction to St. Thomas Aquinas* (New York: The Modern Library, 1948), I q. 13, a. 12, 124.

9. Gustav Bergmann, "Stenius on the *Tractatus*" in *Logic and Reality*, 245.

10. Ibid., "Stenius on the *Tractatus*" in *Logic and Reality*, 245–6.

11. Ludwig Wittgenstein, *Tractatus Logico-Philosophicus*, trans. D. F. Pears & B.F. McGuiness (London: Routledge & Kegan Paul, 1961) 2.03, 13.

12. St. Thomas Aquinas, *On Being and Essence*, trans. A. Maurer (Toronto: Pontifical Institute of Medieval Studies, 1949), Chapter III, 40ff.

13. Ibid., *On Being and Essence*, Chapter III, 41.

14. Ibid., *On Being and Essence*, Chapter III, 42.

15. This distinction is not only Thomistic but also Scotistic. Aquinas holds that while any essence taken in itself is neither numerically one nor many, nonetheless it is one or undivided in definition. What Socrates is is one in definition with what Plato is. Scotus too distinguishes numerical unity and the unity of a specific nature. The latter is a real unity proper to a nature apart from any operation of the mind. The nature that is one in this sense " … is considered by the metaphysician and is expressed through a definition…." See Scotus, Duns, *The Oxford Commentary on the Four Books of the Sentences*, trans. James J. Walsh, in Hyman and Walsh, ed., *Philosophy in the Middle Ages* (Indianapolis: Hackett, 1973) Book II, Distinction III, question 1, 582–86.

16. Wittgenstein speaks of still another kind of space which he calls logical space. See L.Wittgenstein, *Tractatus Logico-Philosophicus*, 1.13, 7; 2.11, 15.

17. Scotus, Duns, *The Oxford Commentary on the Four Books of the Sentences*, in Hyman and Walsh, eds. *Philosophy in the Middle Ages*, 584.

Index

Aristotle, 3, 15, 35, 50, 70, 78, 85, 120; ethics, 91; final causes, 35–37; truth, 50, 57
abstraction, 72
accidents, 19, 20
analogous meaning, 31
artistic knowledge and truth, 62

Beatific Vision, 15
being: as essence, 14; as existence, 14–15; not a genus, 13; participative and non-participative, 64–65; primarily identified with God, 31–33
bare particulars, 121
Bergmann, G., 121, 124
Bradley, F.H., 123, 124

causal proof, 21, 23–25; Kant's critique of, 25; objections and replies, 28–30
conceptualism, 78–79; definition, 120. *See also* universals
consciousness, 15
Copernican revolution, 78. *See also* Kant; conceptualism
cosmological proof. *See* Causal proof
criterion, puzzle of, 5

Descartes, 70
dilemma of predication, 72
dilemma of virtue, 102; solution of, 105
divine Ideas, 64–65

dualism, 75; Edwards, Jonathan, 39
epiphenomenalism, 76–77
epistemology, 1
equivocity, 57
essence: as the possible, 14, 15; relative to existence, 14; what a definition signifies, 14. *See also* being; existence
ethics, 1, 2; and virtue, 11; first practical science, 10, 97–98; first principles of, 96; object of, 1
exemplification, 122–123
existence: distinct from essence, 14, 86; not a predicate, 13, 26; reciprocity with essence, 15; relative to existentialism, 16–17; relative to rationalism, 16. *See also* being; essence
existential neutrality: in judgment, 22; in things, 23
existential operator, 17
existentialism, 16–17; Thomistic, 14–16

falsehood, 59–60. *See also* truth
final cause: Aristotle's defense of, 35–37; explains immanent activity, 39–43

Galileo, 35, 78
goodness: as end or goal, 49; compared with truth, 49–54; independent of minds, 50

Hoernle, R.F.A., 78. *See also* conceptualism; Kant
human soul: Aquinas's compromise, 86–88; form of the body, 84; independent of the body, 80–83; paradox in Aquinas, 85–88
Hume, 29–30
hypothetical imperatives, 108–110

idealism, 74
identity materialism, 69–70, 74
immanent activity, 37, 38, 39; implies final cause, 39–43
immutation, 82
infinite regress: Bradley's, 123; Plato's, 121; Ryle's, 122–123
intentionality, 51, 72; and goodness, 52–53; and truth, 51–52
intrinsic vice, 101

James, William, 5

Kant, Immanuel: and the causal proof, 25–26; conceptualism, 78–79; on existence, 13, 26; universalization in ethics, 106, 107–110
knowledge, 61–63, 80–83. *See also* truth

Locke, John, 109
logic, 2
logical positivism, 4, 7

metaphysics, 3; defense of, 6–8; objections to, 3, 5
mind-body issue, 74–80. *See also* dualism; epiphenomenalism
moralism, 115

natural law ethics, 93, 94, 105–107; definition of, 92; ground of universalization, 107–110; in persons, 99; related definitions, 111–112
nominalism, 79; definition, 120. *See also* conceptualism; universals

ought: and natural law ethics, 92–93; defined in terms of end, 93

passive intellect, 81, 83

persons, 10, 69–70; and logic, 70–77
Plato: his idea of a person, 70; separated universals, 121; the Demiurge, 65; "third-man" objection, 119; unchangeable nature of Forms, 73
powers, 86, 88
practical science, 97–98
predicable relations, 70–72; and mind-body issue, 74
prima facie duties, 110–111
primal matter, 65
Pyrrho, 5

realism: Aristotelian, 120; extreme, 120; moderate, 120; scholastic, 120, 126; vs. nominalism and conceptualism, 77–80
right reason, 100
Russell, B., 120
Ryle G., 122. *See also* infinite regress

Saint Anselm, 56
Saint Augustine, 56
Sartre, 16
Schmidt R. W., 89n2
science: objects of, 1; practical vs. theoretical, 96
scientism, 115
Scotus, 128n15
second intentions, 78. *See also* predicable relations
Spinoza, 28
Stallknecht, N.P., 79
substance, 19, 20

teleology, 39–43. *See also* final cause
theory of types, 123, 124. *See also* infinite regress
transitive activity, 37. *See also* immanent activity
truth: Aquinas's broader definition, 60; as known, 63; identified primarily with God, 64–65; non-propositional, 59; of judgments, 55; practical vs. theoretical, 55; relation to knowledge, 61–63; three divisions of, 60; two sides of, 54

universalization, 107
universals, 119, 120; Thomistic view, 126–127. *See also* conceptualism;

realism
utilitarianism, 110

Veatch H. B., 89n2
virtue, 11; as mean, 100. *See also* dilemma of virtue

Wittgenstein, 124, 128n16

Zeno, 123